HACK PROOF YOUR BUSINESS

Volume 2

Featuring 14 IT Experts
Nationwide

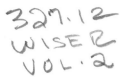

Hack Proof Your Business Volume 2 Copyright © 2020 Chris Wiser.

Disclaimer: This book is designed to provide general information for our readers. It is sold with the understanding that the publisher is not engaged to render any type of legal, business or any other kind of professional advice. The content of each chapter is the sole expression and opinion of its author, and not necessarily that of the publisher. No warranties or guarantees are expressed or implied by the publisher's choice to include any of the content in this volume. Neither the publisher nor the individual author(s) shall be liable for any physical, psychological, emotional, financial, or commercial damages, including, but not limited to, special, incidental, consequential or other damages. The reader is responsible for their own choices, actions, and results.

Prominence Publishing
www.prominencepublishing.com

Hack Proof Your Business Volume 2/Chris Wiser. -- 1st ed.
ISBN 978-1-988925-55-4

Contents

Foreword

By Chris Wiser

The number one threat to businesses today is a cybersecurity breach. Small business owners can no longer afford to turn a blind eye, thinking, "It won't happen to me." The thieves are out there, targeting all kinds of businesses, large and small. No one is immune to it. They may hack into your system and steal your confidential data, they might freeze your phone systems, or they might hold all your customers' data ransom and demand that you pay. Every day a new threat emerges.

It's time to take IT seriously. For those of us who work in the IT industry, it's astounding how many small business owners think that they are meeting their IT needs, when in fact, they are surprisingly lacking in even the basic security. They are leaving gaping holes through which the criminals can step right in. It's essentially an open invitation for the thieves, who are getting smarter and smarter each passing day.

Right now, the best thing that business owners can do is to have a business threat mitigation plan in place, but even more importantly, have a dedicated IT person (or team) who is highly skilled in Cybersecurity.

It's not a matter of "if" a breach will happen, it's when.

For the most part, all businesses rely on technology on a day-to-day basis. Can you imagine what would happen to your business if the required technology was no longer available?

If you are a business owner, it is CRUCIAL that you take IT seriously. Budget, plan and execute.

We have put together 'Hack Proof Your Business, Volume 2' in an effort to educate and advocate for small business owners. We've gathered a group of IT & Cybersecurity Specialists from across North America to explain the various aspects of Cybersecurity and what you can do to protect your business and your livelihood from cybersecurity threats.

Remember, NO BUSINESS is too small to avoid this, and you need to prepare.

Chris Wiser,

CEO, 7 Figure MSP

Speaker/Trainer/ Entrepreneur Coach

Building Cyber-Security Awareness Into Your Company Culture

By Bill Bunnell

Your business is under attack, and your employees are the target of these attacks. Many business owners believe that cybersecurity is purely a technical issue—resolved through technological means by adding antivirus software, upgrading to a better firewall, or employing the newest technology for preventing cyber attacks. More and more, the focus of these attacks is the employees that work for you. You may ask yourself, "Why would anyone want to attack my business?" According to the Verizon Data Breach Investigations Report of 2019, 43% of all breaches involved small business victims.[1] In addition, 39% of all breaches came from organized criminal groups. Of those, 71% were financially motivated, and—the

---

[1] https://enterprise.verizon.com/resources/reports/2019-data-breach-investigations-report.pdf

scariest of all the statistics—56% of these breaches took months or longer to discover.

The fact is, your business is an easy target, and criminals focus on where they can most likely succeed. Another key statistic showing that your employees are the focus of these attacks is that 94% of all attacks are delivered directly to a user's email inbox. This book discusses lots of ways that you can go about protecting your business, some technical and others more common sense. Whichever combination of techniques you use, it is paramount to build a company culture that includes a focus on cybersecurity.

As an IT professional with over 20 years of industry experience and as CEO of Network Builders IT, my job, along with my team, is to educate and protect our customers regarding the risks associated with cybersecurity. In this chapter, I will disucss why it is important that a company culture includes a focus on cybersecurity, and the key components that will help make your security successful.

Why CyberSecurity Should Be Part of Your Corporate Culture

As with any major business objective, there are three significant areas that need examination; they are illustrated below in the People - Process - Technology triangle.

Often, cybersecurity is looked at as part of the Process or Technology pillar, but as I stated previously, current attacks focus on your employees and the people that work for you. Therefore, the People pillar should receive adequate focus to ensure that objectives are met. Often, when only one or two of the three pillars are addressed, headline-making breaches happen. The most effective way to address the People pillar is to build cybersecurity into the company culture. Let's discuss some of the individual components that you can implement to help build security into your company dynamics.

What is Company Culture?

Let's start by defining what "company culture" means. This is sometimes hard to answer because if you ask ten people to describe what company culture means to them, you will most likely end up with ten different answers. Typically, you will hear words like "glue," "magic," "atmosphere," or "DNA." When looking in the dictionary, there is no definition for "company culture," and when looking to Wikipedia, organizational culture is defined as the "behavior of humans within an organization and the meaning that people attach to those behaviors." What the heck does that even mean? Company culture, to me, is the way we treat our fellow employees, clients, and prospects, the goals of our business, and what is deemed wrong or right in reaching those goals. Finally, I believe company culture includes activities and/or responsibilities that the company considers important for the survival of their business. This is where cybersecurity comes in. Without it, a business is at risk.

The reality is, modifying an existing company's culture is not something that can happen overnight. It takes time, dedication, and commitment. Now, let's discuss the necessary steps to building the security-focused culture we need.

Outlining the Goal

It is important to verbalize the goals of cybersecurity to our employees. Why are we focused on it, and what do we hope to gain by building a cybersecurity culture? The ability to clearly communicate an organization's cybersecurity mission and goals will help everyone buy into the need to help and understand why each person's role is important.

To start, it is important to understand what we are trying to accomplish. In a company that has a strong security culture, when the employees discover something that is out of the ordinary or suspicious, they know to whom they should report this information. In a company that has a weak security culture, the feeling is that security is someone else's responsibility and there is no shared sense of ownership to protect the business from risk. Adding security as part of your company's culture can be done in many ways.

Establishing Leadership Support

Company culture comes from the top-down. If the leaders of an organization do not believe in the importance of developing a cybersecurity culture, employees will see that, and in return, not put forth a true effort. The number one step in building a security culture in your business is leadership support. Leaders must clearly communicate where the company is today with its security initiatives and what the company is trying to achieve. Frequent reporting is another crucial step in which leaders are reporting, for example, on security awareness training, or where the company is having success.

Establishing Employee Support

The risk of a headline-making breach may not feel like a real threat to some of the departments in your business so it is essential to earn employee support at all levels of the company. One way of building support is by having conversations and talking to your employees about the impact of cybersecurity. Discuss the fact that threats could exist for the company and cybersecurity may affect employees and customers. Once employees understand the risks and how they can affect not only themselves but the rest of the organization, employees are much more willing to jump on board and participate.

Many employees see their job as nontechnical, and because of this, they don't realize or believe that their role can affect a company's security. The perception of having a nontechnical job can lead to employees letting their guard down, not looking for potential attacks. Companies need to educate their employees by explaining the role they each play in cybersecurity and the risks associated with their jobs. Employees need to be taught why cybersecurity is important, what impact poor cybersecurity can have on an organization, and what employees can do to prevent issues. Here are a few examples of things that can be done to accomplish corporate safety.

Security Awareness Training

With security awareness training, it is important that employees are not given pure theory. Provide relatable lessons directly applicable to an employee's job—use real-life, illustrative examples. In addition, ensure that the training does not interrupt the employee's daily workflow.

Test Security Posture

The easiest way to test your security posture is by using phishing campaigns within your organization or other social engineering testing campaigns. Running test phishing campaigns gives your employees the ability to test their knowledge and awareness, detect suspicious activities, and most importantly, practice reporting suspicious activities to the appropriate people in the company. When employees fail testing campaigns, it is essential to inform the employees what information could have been breached and how to protect the information moving forward. At the beginning of a testing campaign, it is very important not to punish underperforming test results, but support, coach, and train the employees to do better moving forward.

Continuous Communication

Immediate communication and follow-through are important when employees communicate suspicious activity. Employees need to know that you take cybersecurity very seriously, that it is indeed a shared responsibility across all employees of the organization. Also, be sure to share your findings with the rest of the company. Being able to use real-world examples that occurred within your business is a sure way to reinforce that cybersecurity is important and a real threat.

Education and Awareness

Companies must ensure that employees know why it is important to care about cybersecurity. It is important that training and education are not only focused on the business's risks, but employees should also be taught how to improve their cybersecurity skills when using personal devices. As technology becomes a bigger part of our lives and jobs, the lines and boundaries of where we access company data are blurred. Many people access their work email from their personal computers and cell phones. If an employee is accessing work email from home and has poor cybersecurity on their own personal electronics, their company can be at risk. Some specific subjects on which to educate employees are the following:

- The need for strong, unique passwords: Require your employees to use strong passwords that are at least 12 characters long, and are complex—using numeric, uppercase, lowercase, and special characters.

- The risks associated with public wireless networks and the need for Virtual Private Networks (VPN).

- How to spot suspicious activities.

It is important that training is not a one-time effort. To really become part of the company culture, cybersecurity training needs to happen often to ensure employees don't become relaxed or complacent.

In conclusion, it is important that companies keep vigilant because of our world's evolving security threats. It is not safe to try and rely on technology alone to protect our businesses; we also need to address our People—employees are the biggest liability (and asset) that we have. The best approach is to develop a company culture where every employee takes responsibility for protecting the business. Develop a strong cybersecurity culture where everyone understands the risks and rewards.

A company must go to great lengths to help protect itself and its assets. If this is something you feel you need help with, make sure you find an experienced IT company. Find a company with a focus on cybersecurity who can provide your company with clear guidelines for helping you walk through the cybersecurity culture process and build a solid one.

Remember that addressing security is not a one-time event. You cannot train your employees once and assume you're protected. It is something that needs continual attention through the life of your business.

About the Author

Bill Bunnell is the Founder and CEO of Network Builders IT Inc., a Managed IT Services company and Founder and CEO of Cyberr Inc., a Managed Security Services Provider. Mr. Bunnell has over 20 years of experience in the IT industry. For the majority of those years, Mr. Bunnell has worked as a consultant providing network support for clients. Clients ranging from small to medium sized businesses to city governments, and publicly traded companies. Bill's roles have included project and technical lead for domestic and international mergers, global Microsoft Exchange design and implementations, and data center virtualization.

As CEO of Network Builders IT, Mr. Bunnell has built an award-winning IT company. Network Builders IT, IT has been named as one of the top 501 Managed Service Providers in the world in 2019 and 2015. In 2019 Network Builders IT was named to the Inc. 5000 list as one of the fastest-growing companies in America. Also, Network Builders IT, has won several industry awards from CRN and The Channel Company including the following awards, Tech Elite 250 and Next Gen 250 in 2018 and Next Gen 250 in 2017.

Network Builders IT is focused on providing the best IT services and practices while using the best technologies. Mr. Bunnell founded Network Builders IT with the specific goal to bring flat-rate managed IT services to the local market. Having been successful with that goal, Mr. Bunnell is now focused on providing Managed cyber security services through Cyberr Inc., and better protecting business. As today's security landscape changes dramatically, it becomes increasingly complex and costly to protect a business.

If you have questions about Cyber Security or Managed IT Services, Mr. Bunnell is available to speak with you. Go to https://nbit.com/help-protect-my-business, to up a time to discuss your questions and needs.

Anatomy of a Hacker

By Chuck Tomlinson

We live in a predominantly digital world, and the nuts and bolts that make it click are hidden in plain sight—behind the screens of the devices that we use. These physical objects carry the software that runs our newsfeeds, defines our daily schedule, runs our businesses and—designed to be as hassle-free as possible— are immune to power outages, running even in the event of a natural disaster. These systems are, however, quite susceptible to human-made issues that can have a decidedly negative effect on our lives, either through ignorance or via malicious intent.

As we will see, these two elements together can incur a lot of damage, turning a prosperous company into a digital Titanic, a force completely unaware that a destructive iceberg is directly in its path. The architect of this disaster isn't someone on the ship, in this case, an employee. It is often a person that is faceless and nameless, enjoying complete anonymity off the ship, and defined only by the result of their efforts.

Financial incentive has long been the primary motivator for hacking attacks; it is estimated that the global cost of damages incurred by hacking attacks will amount to a whopping six trillion dollars by 2021[2]. However, the past decade has shown trends that surpass mere financial damage, showcasing ideological liabilities as well as propaganda wars between nation-states. North Korea is known to have backed hacking groups involved in attacks against international banking services, compromising an untold number of machines, stealing hundreds of millions of dollars in the process.[3] It is clear that in the event of a global crisis, some of the most coveted soldiers will be those seated in comfortable office chairs.

The 2010s was the decade of the smartphone,[4] a device that provided unprecedented access to the internet, along with a complete revamp of how we consume media. Everyone became connected, leading to unique, unparalleled marketing opportunities. Where businesses saw possibilities, others saw prey: consumers who were unprepared or ambivalent, those carrying compromised devices wherever they went, including their work environment. Everything became an opportunity, because everyone carried a liability with them wherever they went.

---

[2] This is according to research conducted by Cybersecurity Ventures – doubling the damages from 2015. https://cybersecurity ventures.com/hackerpocalypse-cybercrime-report-2016/

[3] As reported by https://www.reuters.com/article/us-northkorea-usa-sanctions-idUSKCN1VY1RB - the most disturbing among these developments being the attack on Britain's National Health Service.

[4] The unprecedented accessibility came with its own set of (dis)advantages. https://finance.yahoo.com/news/decade-review-smartphone-wrought-171946247.html

To understand cybersecurity and hacking, we must understand the people who commit these actions.

Toying With the System: Engineering the Employees

A hacker is, by definition, an opportunist. A loner by nature, craving company, only to multiply the knowledge obtained through long solitary hours spent bathed in the cold glare of a computer screen. Accruing knowledge and probing the vulnerabilities in closed systems isn't the type of work that appeals to those who want to program sleek apps with all their bells and whistles.

Whistling That Works

Speaking of whistles, back in the day, even a plastic one—a mere child's toy found in a cereal box— could signal trouble for a major corporation. If a whistle's finder knew both the technical engineering of the telephone system and how the whistle's particular sound pitch could disrupt it, they could create a hack into the phone system. As a university student in 1972, John Draper figured out that whistling at a precise, 2600Hz frequency creates a tone that allows a person to place toll-free phone calls.[5] He and his group managed to find a holy grail of communication. Once figured

---

[5] https://www.dailydot.com/layer8/john-draper-captain-crunch/
The group quickly moved from the Cap'n Crunch toy whistle and built their own blue box device and trying to sell it, which led to their downfall.

out, the exploit was easy to reproduce, since no AT&T engineer had thought to create a prevention against such outside factors. A careless media interview pinpointed the threat, and with millions on the line, the FBI got involved, resulting in Draper's arrest for toll fraud.

Gentleman Hacker

Like no other hacker before or since, Kevin Mitnick embodied the quintessential confidence trickster. His most famous exploits weren't aimed at the general population, but instead dealt with employees of large tech companies: people that should have known better. Actually, it is precisely these employees' knowledge that turned them into perfect targets. The employees would receive an innocuous call during their shift, from a person who told them he was an engineer, saturating the conversation with highly technical terms that surely only an engineer and staff person would understand. The employee would then be asked to do something simple enough, like read a number printed on the modem in front of them. Just like that, the company was compromised, without the employee knowing the power that they just given to the nice person on the other end of the line.

Mitnick and Draper helped form the hacker archetype and influenced generations of computer nerds raised on the mythology woven around their exploits. This is where the problem lies; it's easy to see the draw hacker culture has on young people—

its promise of freedom, revolt against the corporate order, and a think-outside-the-box mentality. Never before was breaking the law so fun, so impersonal. You could steal sensitive data or exploit the system for your needs without physically breaking into company offices and victims were just words in the newspaper stories. However, the law saw it differently. Soon, it became clear that each hacker had to choose between a career in security or a life spent on the run.

Tools, Trends, and Terminology

A hacker is capable of circumventing software limitations and is far from a simple user of suspicious programs. By being able to reverse engineer the code at hand, a savvy hacker will repurpose the digital object and turn it into something its original creators did not foresee. The terminology associated with the scene is too numerous to count, but several key areas threaten users and companies today. They include:

- **Botnets**: these represent vast clusters of zombie machines, hijacked by malicious programs, and used in denial of service (DDoS) attacks against websites. It's easy to imagine how this affects businesses built around the online distribution model. The owners of these botnet networks are usually far from the legal jurisdiction of the country where the attacked businesses resides, so many victim businesses have no other recourse than to pay a monthly sum for conducting their business in peace. This type of racketeering proves especially devious and hard to solve since many businesses are discouraged from reporting it to authorities; the geography of the online world is traversed in an instant, an advantage quickly turned into a nightmare for those unlucky enough to be caught in the sights of a botnet attack.

- **Phishing and its variants**: An old technique, made mainstream famous by the Nigerian e-mail scammers,[6] phishing relies on human greed and carelessness in equal measure. It is the most famous and the most effective form of social engineering, through millions of e-mails sent to users daily. Many of these emails are intentionally poorly worded, to further narrow the search for those gullible enough to go along with the lucrative chances the fake messages offer. Others mimic trusted institutions such as banks and social networks, obtaining login data, credit card numbers, and other sensitive information. The best answer to phishing attempts is vigilance, but what seems simple on paper isn't easy to conduct in reality.

---

[6] Typical scams are deliberately designed around nebulous proposals, with new iterations being devised on a yearly basis. https://www.scamwatch.gov.au/types-of-scams/unexpected-money/nigerian-scams

Today, corporations spend billions on employee awareness courses, repeating these drills to lower the chance of a costly data breach.

- **Malicious programs, or malware**: This is an umbrella term for software that inflicts intentional damage to a home or business system. Many of these programs manage to tread a fine line and stay within legal limits, overloading a system with aggressive ad campaigns, and redirecting online search results to businesses involved in the scheme. Adware and spyware programs are notoriously hard to remove and can be a cause of endless annoyance, even to those with a higher degree of computer literacy. Others, like viruses and trojan horses, serve to hijack a computer system completely, steal sensitive information, or wipe the disk clean for no other reason than to create damage. To achieve the greatest effect possible, these rely on zero-day exploits, unpatched vulnerabilities of which system administrators are unaware.

These persistent trends speak volumes about the continuous growth of the internet and the huge potential it has as a global marketplace. These trends also clearly show that rather than resorting to intricate schemes, most hacking groups prefer to use blunt digital tools, casting a wide net that often produces the best monetary results. With the entire world coming online, we become locked in an uphill struggle based around continuous education of the average user and the endless patching of vulnerabilities, all in the name of loss prevention.

Parting the Cloud

Software as a service (SaaS) represents one of the most popular forms of software licensing present today. Closely associated with cloud computing, it brings personal and company data online and easily implements a subscription model that enables steady revenue flow. Data is stored on remote servers, guarded by the hosting company's protocols. Applications are also licensed at a favorable price, often with company discounts. This trend took the online world by storm and is already a market force that cannot be ignored for most online businesses.[7]

This outlook turned SaaS providers into prime targets for various hacking attempts. In 2016, Dropbox announced that more than sixty-eight million user passwords were stolen four years previously.[8] This lax approach to security from a cloud storage provider cast serious doubts on the industry's capabilities to protect its users and their login information. The announcement followed

[7] https://www.gartner.com/en/newsroom/press-releases/2019-04-02-gartner-forecasts-worldwide-public-cloud-revenue-to-g
[8] https://www.theguardian.com/technology/2016/aug/31/dropbox-hack-passwords-68m-data-breach

with a reiteration of security drills, but for many, it was too little, too late. The renewed interest in proper data encryption was the silver lining of the situation, and the SaaS model continued to grow. Heightened user awareness became the bottom line around which companies rallied their customers. This made the job of "White Hat" hackers—administrators and security consultants, those who probe a system to patch its vulnerabilities—a tiny bit easier as a result.

Adversaries or Allies?

The "Black Hat" vs. "Gray Hat" debate has been going on for a long time in online circles; many hackers caught by law enforcement agencies found jobs in national security, as their skills were too important to waste on prison sentences. It is, therefore, possible—with a legal or financial incentive—to convert even the most hardened digital criminal. But can they really be trusted?

The best answer is: *most likely, yes*. The romanticized depiction of hackers in media isn't without a grain of truth. Sometimes, they are portrayed as mavericks that figuratively scale corporate towers and eventually reach the hard decision between darkness and compromise. On the other hand, companies can learn to be more than mere targets, adjusting their HR drives and marketing campaigns to project an outward image of a tech-aware employer, offering lucrative careers to those that would otherwise feel out of place in the job market. This intention instills a sense of security within the customer base, showing that the company is well-adjusted to the requirements put forth by ever-changing digital trends.

Today, the IT department is a necessary part of company structure. Modern employees use at least several applications in both their personal and professional life and expect to be provided with secure data protocols. The core question is the way a company chooses to protect its portfolio and employees—by hoping that the breach will not occur, or by hiring people that will test the waters and report the findings.[9] By embracing a flexible perspective, a business can finally bring together the inquisitive nature of a hacker's mind and the company's need for security.

This new business outlook is closely tied to the emergence of managed security service providers (MSSP). Smart businesses are partnering with companies like mine that provide outsourced IT protection services. This development enables small businesses to obtain a comparable level of network security to their large corporate counterparts, at a fraction of the cost. Online components have made custom-fit solutions possible. Round-the-clock monitoring and the expertise needed to set up system procedures that react to perceived threats in real-time are thanks to the instant implementation of updates. Hackers are, after all, involved in the industry that prides

---

[9] https://www.cbsnews.com/news/companies-hire-hackers-to-break-into-their-systems/

itself on adaptability, and the positive flux an MSSP produces shows how proactively dealing with risk can serve to embrace change and strengthen a company's structure. By implementing these changes to your business model, you will join a thriving marketplace of ideas, where investing in security means obtaining future opportunities.

About the Author

With over 20 years of IT experience, Chuck Tomlinson has watched as technology rapidly changed.

In his early years in technology, Chuck served eight years in the United States Air Force as an F-15 Fighter Jet Avionics Technician while also working as a network administrator for his Squadron and the local Lockheed Martin members at Tyndall Air Force Base.

In 2001, Chuck founded Spectrumwise in Charlotte, North Carolina, with the vision to help small and medium-sized businesses get a real return on their technology investments. Spectrumwise has remained dedicated to providing state-of-the-art IT support, Cybersecurity threat mitigation, Disaster Recovery, and business VOIP phone systems to allow its clients to get ahead of the competition and achieve greater success.

Chuck welcomes you to contact Spectrumwise today at 704-527-8324 or visit his website at www.spectrumwise.com to discover how he can design, create, and implement an IT strategy with your unique business in mind.

When Chuck isn't busy with his many on-going IT projects, he enjoys his downtime with his wife Susan and tries to achieve life balance. He also enjoys music and plays piano and keyboards regularly with his church's worship team.

"It won't happen to me!" The True Cyber Threat to Small Businesses

By Chuck Brown

"Dear Customer. Your Antivirus protection has expired. This Email is in regard of your computer network security and your email ID abc@zzzzzz.com."

That was the beginning of an email I received from one of our long-term clients, forwarded along with the question, "Is this legit? Should I click on the link?"

As CEO of one of the oldest and largest Managed Services Providers in the Low Country, I've seen emails like this before. Fortunately, this client knew the signs of a scam and also knew to contact us whenever he was the least bit suspicious. Unfortunately, not everyone contacts their MSP when they receive these types of scams.

My name is Chuck Brown and I'm CEO of Infinity, Inc. Our company prides itself on providing strategic direction and solutions for our clients' information technology infrastructure. We value developing long-term relationships with our clients, working with small and medium-sized businesses on everything from the nuts and bolts of designing and implementing networks, to building unified communications strategies, to workflow and surveillance. It is our job to make sure the technology our clients use supports their business goals rather than hinders them.

We have been providing IT consulting and management in the Savannah, Georgia area since 1999. Over that time, our focus has changed quite a bit. Security was the last thing on the list when we started out; it was hard enough just getting connected, so there was very little thought to security. Even back then, however, it mattered.

Remember the movie War Games with Matthew Broderick? The "threat" was a young geek with a noisy modem trying to call into random phone numbers looking for computer games. Well, suffice it to say that the threat has **evolved**. Businesses now face much more sophisticated threats than a school kid—with tools that are far more advanced than Broderick's character had.

With no end to the malicious tools available for attacking your network, one of the biggest security problems facing small businesses today is complacency.

There is often an attitude of "it won't happen to me" which prevents small business owners from taking even the smallest steps to protect themselves. There is a misconception that "I'm not a worthwhile target" which leads to a false sense of security. This kind of thinking is not only dangerous, but irresponsible, as some preventive steps are not that costly, and the cost of doing nothing can be extremely high.

~

Let's take a look at the numbers. The Hiscox 2018 Small Business Cyber Risk Report shows that 47% of small businesses suffered at least one cyber attack in the past twelve months.

If you knew that there was a 47% chance that someone would try to break into your office this year, wouldn't you rethink your physical security? Add on an extra padlock, access code, or sensor? At the very least, find out how many keys might be floating around and who might have them?

That is truly what small businesses face today. The threat is from within the organization and from outside, digital and physical. And before I share the secrets of our successful security strategy, let's dispel a few more myths.

Myth #1 - The data I have isn't valuable. Perhaps. But there are a lot of reasons you might be breached. First, keep in mind that many network attacks are opportunistic, not targeted. It's like a car thief walking down the street and checking to see who left their doors unlocked, rather than specifically looking for a BMW to heist. Just because your data isn't important to someone else doesn't mean it's not important to you. If it has value to you, a hacker knows that there's probably a price you'd pay to keep it intact.

Then again, you may have more value than you realize stored in your network. Any names and email addresses? How about the social security numbers of your team? Any information on your pricing structure that you wouldn't want a competitor to have? Everyone has something with value, either to themselves or someone else.

Myth #2 - Cyber Security is expensive, and the threat just isn't great enough for me to spend the money. Like any security, you can do nothing, you can spend the entire budget, or you can take measures that are consistent with your needs. Most of us don't have bank vault doors at the front of our houses—it's overkill. However, most of us also don't have a simple, bedroom door-style, push-button lock on the front door, either. We use keys and sometimes deadbolts. Network security is the same way. Evaluate your risk, evaluate how you can best mitigate that risk, then make intelligent decisions on the best way to protect your company.

Myth #3 - It won't happen to me. You might be right. But if you're wrong, the damage could put you out of business or worse. Remember that decreasing your risk doesn't have to be an expensive proposition.

There are many security myths that could impact your decision-making process. For more information, check out our blog post at https://www.infinityinc.us/top-10-cybersecurity-misconceptions-of-smbs/

~

I'm going to cover a few concrete things you can do to protect yourself a little later in this chapter. However, the title of this chapter is "The True Cyber Threat to Small Business" so let's dig into why all of this should concern you first.

For many of us, the threat is much greater than the loss of some data. If you have good backups and a solid plan, you can have assurance that your data will be recoverable. "Well, if I get my data back, why should I care about all of this?" Glad you asked! Here are a few scenarios you might want to consider.

Scenario 1: You come into work Monday morning and before you log in, someone tells you that the network is acting strangely. They've tried to open files that seem like they are corrupted. Turns out they've been hit by malware.

If you're lucky, the malware is isolated to this one computer. If you're not, it has spread to your network. Unfortunately, different attacks act differently. Some may display a message, some may spread from computer to computer; it all depends on how it's coded, how your users respond, and how your network is set up.

If it is isolated quickly, you may minimize the damage. If not, it could take out the whole network. It typically takes time to ascertain what's going on and come up with a plan. If the course of action is to restore from the last complete backup, you will most certainly lose some data (whatever was updated since that last backup), and you'll lose productivity for the time your team can't work. However, if those two things are as bad as it gets, you are in pretty good shape. You've lost a few updates and some time, but you'll recover. If your backups aren't solid, it's a whole different situation.

Scenario 2: You click a link that you thought was about an Amazon shipment… it wasn't. This gave the bad guys access to your extensive email list of contacts and vendors. The script that you accidentally ran on your computer emailed each one of them FROM YOUR EMAIL ADDRESS, asking them to contribute to the "help for homeless Siamese cats" charity that's been set up. Now, most of your friends are pretty smart and will know that you would never ask for such a donation—you hate cats. But a few of them fall for it, and when they click the link to donate, they are also infected.

That's bad enough. But then there is that customer who's particularly security sensitive. He figures that if you have no better control over your network than this, you probably are not secure enough to do business with. Or the email solicited something more embarrassing than cat funds. Or the names and emails were simply collected and sold on the dark web.

No matter the details of this scenario, what is the cost to your business for your tarnished reputation?

Scenario 3: You are a contractor and bid for jobs constantly. One of your team comes into work one day and sees a fancy USB drive in the parking lot. He realizes it's a pretty expensive one and wants to find out to whom it belongs. So, he fires up his computer and plugs in the USB.

Fortunately for the person who "lost" it, there's nothing on it but a couple of photos of a building. Unfortunately for you, when your employee plugged it in, it ran an installer for software that monitors your well-intentioned team member's computer. Now every time he pulls up a bid, a copy of it goes to your competitor. Sound far-fetched? It's not at all. This technique has been around for years, and consistent underbidding could have you out of business in short order.

~

If you're still with me, you now may be horrified. I'm not trying to scare you (well, not really). The risks already exist. We simply need to acknowledge them so we can properly assess them. A good security strategy has to consider a lot of things:

- Your exposure from your staff, both intentional and unintentional

- Natural disasters: fire, flood, storm

- Technology disasters: deleted files, equipment damage, corruption, theft of information, intentional (and unintentional) incorrect changes of information

- Malware attacks such as virus infection, ransomware/encryption and breach resulting in data theft. Such theft can include customer records, intellectual property, customer credit card information, company financials and employee information.

- Website attacks: Your website can be hijacked, sending visitors to a malicious site or incorrect and/or embarrassing information posted to your site

- And this is the tip of the iceberg!

If Matthew Broderick's character in War Games could break into the Department of Defense with a dial-up modem in 1983, what chance do the rest of us have against all of these threats today? How can any small business possibly fund complete and absolute protection of its network assets? In general, you can't. It is not really even possible. Just like the old saying that there is no lock that cannot be broken, there is really no network that cannot be compromised, given enough time and effort.

Large corporations with millions of dollars to spend on security get hacked. City and county governments, power companies, and schools get broken into. For those of us operating a small business, absolute prevention is not the correct approach.

Let's go back and consider the 47% chance of break-in statistic. Most of us have one or more of the following physical protection measures in place:

- Regular key locks on our doors
- Deadbolt locks
- Chain or bar swing locks
- Cameras
- Alarm system
- Guard dog

We use multiple safety measures because the best approach to take is a layered one. A combination of prevention and remediation plans will help protect the integrity of your business.

Let's assume for a moment that you cannot prevent intrusion. Not that we're not going to try, but we're also not going to blow the entire budget on a security plan that, at the end of the day, still isn't absolutely perfect. Instead we're going to develop a reasonable security plan that will go a long way towards preventing most attempts to breach our network. We're going to layer on top of that a reasonably detailed, step-by-step plan that documents what we're going to do if there is a breach. Finally, we're going to spend a lot of effort to make sure we have rock solid backups and a process to ensure that they are secure, complete, and recoverable.

These three basic layers will significantly decrease your vulnerability. There are others you can include to increase your security further. With the right planning, the effect on your operations if something does happen can be minimized to the point where it becomes a concern you think about, but not one you worry about. There is a HUGE difference between the two.

~

I could write a whole book on security for small businesses, but the goal here is to give you a starting point. Here are a few, really important, general considerations for a great layered security plan:

1. Use a business-class firewall to separate your network from the internet.

2. Use a commercial anti-virus solution on every server and user computer. The free stuff is better than nothing, but the rule of "you get what you pay for" applies here.

3. Have appropriate security policies enforced on your network. These include password complexity and change policies (there are a variety of thoughts on what works best; the

intent here is not to cover WHAT the policies should be, rather that they should EXIST).

4. Implement access policies for your data. Give staff access to only the things they need in order to significantly cut down on what can be damaged.

5. Have good backups. Understand how often your backups are made, how long they are kept, and what it takes to restore from "bare metal" (meaning if you start with a new server, what it takes to completely restore your environment). Are your backups tested? How often? A backup plan that's never tested is only marginally better than no backups at all. You have something you think you can rely on, but that's a false security.

6. Train your users.

7. Train your users.

8. Train your users. Seem redundant? It's one of the most important pieces. By far, more networks are damaged by users clicking where they shouldn't, opening emails that they shouldn't, and visiting websites that they shouldn't, than anything else. Most of the time, they really didn't know better. Most of your team wants to do the right thing, they just don't always know what that is. This is not intensive education and it doesn't require an IT degree to understand. Teach them to ask first, click second. Teach them to

let someone know if they think they've clicked where they shouldn't. It's very much in your favor if your employees are empowered to ask about something suspicious rather than hide things in fear that they've done something wrong. The faster you know there's a problem, the more options you have for dealing with it.

Hopefully, you now have a sense of how important cyber safety is to the continued health of your company. This chapter is not intended to frighten you—more importantly, it's to educate you on the necessity of paying attention to data security.

There are tons of tools and techniques to help protect the assets of your business. A seasoned technology company can be invaluable in navigating those options, helping you to develop a reasonable security and backup strategy.

If your company has between 10 and 250 workstations and you would like to discuss network security strategy, please give us a call at Infinity for a free consultation. No cost, no contracts, no sales pitch. Just a discussion about where you are and how you might implement some changes that will help you sleep better at night! Call (912) 629-2426 and mention this book. It's that easy.

About the Author

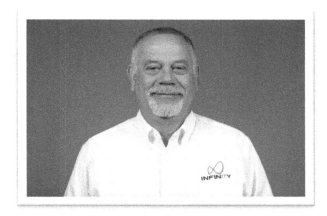

With more than 30 years of experience in computer network support, IT consulting, and running his own company, Chuck Brown knows the key to developing effective business technology solutions.

He is the CEO of Infinity, Inc., an award-winning managed services provider in Savannah that he co-founded with his brother, David. Together they have been providing strategy and support of enterprise-class information services for small and medium-sized businesses since 1999.

Chuck has been recognized as a Coastal Expert by WSAV and appeared on WTOC as a cybersecurity expert, as well as being featured on various podcasts.

He and David pride themselves on building relationships and providing straightforward counsel to businesses throughout Georgia and South Carolina. By focusing on solving business issues, they and the team at Infinity deliver peace of mind and partnership for all the technology your business needs to succeed. Connect with Chuck at https://www.infinityinc.us.

Cyber Safety Best Practices For the Health Care Sector

By Steve Schabacker

Charles Dickens starts out his novel, *A Tale of Two Cities,* by stating, "It was the best of times, it was the worst of times." This statement holds true today, especially concerning the practice of modern medicine. New technology such as stem cell treatments, 3D printing, and genome therapy have allowed new ways to treat patients. The use of electronic health records (EHR) and the internet allow physicians to collaborate like never before. With all this great new power also comes great responsibility. Patients trust medical professionals to keep them safe with both their health and their private information.

The first step in fixing any problem is to realize there is a problem. Some health care professionals may say, "I think we are HIPAA compliant, isn't that enough?" Others may think, "Is my patient data safe from hackers? Where do I even start?" These are questions I am commonly asked in my day-today practice at Medicus Technologies. If you are wondering these same things, you are not alone. In this chapter, I hope to answer these questions, as well as provide insight into the right questions to ask your IT support provider. Whether you use an outside company or have an in-house IT employee, the concepts and concerns are the same.

In order to better explain the lens through which I am approaching this problem, let me tell you a bit about our company. My name is Steve Schabacker and I am the CEO of Medicus Technologies Inc. We are a managed services provider out of Chicago, Illinois with over 10 years' experience helping health care practices with an emphasis in cybersecurity. These include physician offices, dental clinics, chiropractors, and therapists—pretty much any health care service that uses EHR for patients. What a managed services provider (MSP) does is become an extension of an organization's practice and handles all things related to information technology. This includes everything from operating a Help Desk for your staff to call when they have computer issues, to securing your network and data, all the way up to acting as your virtual chief information officer (vCIO) to assist in planning for future growth. Specializing in health care gives us the unique ability to understand the practices we work with at a level that most other MSPs can't.

Is HIPAA Compliancy Enough?

Let's start with the most common question we are asked: "As long as we are HIPAA compliant, our patient data is safe, correct?" The answer is a simple, "Absolutely not." An important thing to remember is that the Health Insurance Portability and Accountability Act (HIPAA) was enacted in 1996 and the most recent updates were back in 2013. The requirements may have been enough in 2013, but in 2020 and beyond, they are barely a good start. Cybersecurity has changed dramatically even in just the last year, let alone the last seven years. Hacking attacks have become more common, more sophisticated, and more costly. While there is no amount of protection that is 100% effective (mainly because of the human factor), layers of protection can get close and eliminate your practice from being a sitting duck.

Thus far, we have established that HIPAA standards are not enough, and your patient data is most likely not secure. You are probably asking yourself "Why should I care?" If you are HIPAA compliant and are meeting that standard, you can't be fined, right? While that may be true, it is not all that matters in this case. Two major concerns come to mind. First off, is trust. How long has it taken you to build trust with your patients and create your practice's reputation? Your patients trust you to care for them—keeping their private data safe is part of that responsibility. Secondly, not securing your practice can cost you a lot of money. In the event of a breach and loss of PHI, the typical cost to a practice averaged $429 per patient file and the average record loss per breach is in the thousands.[10] As you can see, this can add up to a large expenditure. In addition to breaches, ransomware attacks are also common. A ransomware attack typically encrypts all of your files so you cannot access them without paying the hackers a ransom, typically in the hundreds of thousands of dollars.

You are probably thinking "Steve, those don't sound like any fun to deal with." Let me assure you, they are not. While no book, webinar, or whitepaper is going to secure your network for you, I am going to share the six best tips I give the practices with whom we work. These six tips will not fix anything by merely learning them, but with implementation, they can make a huge difference in a health care practice's security.

Tip Number One: establish a security culture. Establishing a security culture starts with employee training. Every member of your team must be aware of cybersecurity's importance. The value of cybersecurity must be applied and enforced on everyone—from your providers all the way to clerical help. Processes, policies, and procedures must be put in place to ensure compliance. Without the right foundation, nothing else can be added to help keep your practice

---

[10] https://www.hipaajournal.com/2019-cost-of-a-databreach-study-healthcare-data-breach-costs/

secure. There is a human factor in almost every breach, and this must be addressed first. Your team of employees and how they conduct themselves has the power to either protect your practice or cause it harm.

Tip Number Two: use strong passwords and change them regularly. Passwords should always be a minimum of eight characters and include at least lower- and upper-case letters, at least one number, and at least one special character. The longer and more complex, the better. Passwords should be changed regularly. We suggest changing them at least every 30 days. Passwords should not be duplicated and used for multiple sites or multiple pieces of software. Users should not share logins or passwords. All that being said, we know that it is very difficult to remember so many passwords, to change them often, and make them complex. That is why we recommend password management software which includes two-factor authentication. This software remembers all your passwords for you, making life easier but also more secure. Two-factor authentication is the key to ensuring your password vault stays secure.

We often hear in the news about "hacks" that are nothing more than someone reusing passwords that were part of a data breach years ago and are available on the dark web. Hackers simply try common sites with these credentials and often get access to your information. One example of this is the recent news story about someone gaining access to a person's Ring account. With this access, the perpetrators were able to view a camera in the house and even talk to the person's children.[11] The news story tried to blame Ring but it was not a breach on Ring's part, it was simply the cybercriminal reusing a password that had been part of a breach and was found on the dark web.

Tip Number Three: limit physical and network access. Physical access means someone being able to touch one of your computers or servers. If someone can physically touch your servers or network equipment, you could be in trouble. Having physical access makes getting into your network very easy. We suggest simple steps like locking the doors to which servers or network equipment reside, and only allow access to personnel that must service the equipment. Swipe card access would be a bonus, keeping a log of who goes in and out. In the event of a breach, an access log provides a useful trail for investigators.

Network access is the ability for a person to get their computer on your network. We would suggest only allowing devices onto your network that must join for work purposes. Employee phones and tablets can become a path for hackers to get into your network if the devices are not properly patched. If you need to provide employees

---

[11] https://www.washingtonpost.com/nation/2019/12/12/she-installed-ring-camera-her-childrens-room-peace-mind-hacker-accessed-it-harassed-her-year-old-daughter

with internet for other devices, we suggest having them on a guest network with physical segregation from your work network.

Tip Number Four: use a next-level antivirus. Traditional antivirus solutions rely upon a library containing millions of signatures, basically pictures of what all known viruses look like. Next-level products such as Sentinel One use behavior-based tracking, focusing on what is happening in the computer. This enables the antivirus software to catch and quarantine new viruses that are not yet on the standard signature library. This is a huge advantage with the ever-changing virus and malware that hackers are constantly evolving. In addition, next-level antivirus also has features that allow a computer to return to a prior state, before an issue happened.

Tip Number Five: choose an IT partner that understands your practice. There are many IT providers out there that are very good at providing general IT services. We recommend going with a firm that specializes in serving your industry. While doctors, dentists, chiropractors, etc. all operate very similarly, they could not be more different in their specific IT and cyber safety needs. Choosing a specialist IT partner can make everything easier: they understand your practice, your needs, your frustrations, and how to best help you plan for the future of your practice. When looking for a partner, we also suggest choosing one with a cybersecurity focus. Unfortunately, we see many IT companies today that still believe IT is as simple as updating Windows and installing an antivirus. Hackers today bring their "A Game." So should your IT company.

Tip Number Six: plan for the unexpected. Today, it is not a matter of *if* something will happen but *when*. Having proper backups in place and a plan to restore them are key. Many different scenarios can happen, including breaches, data thefts, ransomware, fire, or even a natural disaster. How ready is your practice to recover from any of these? Having plans in place for each scenario can make all the difference when something happens. In the event of an emergency, hours can decide the outcome between recovery or catastrophe. No one expects a disaster to happen, but odds are that over time, one or more of them will. Once a plan is in place, we also suggest running a practice recovery to eliminate surprises when a real disaster strikes.

I hope these six tips were beneficial in giving you a start on the path to safety and security for your practice and your patients. The path to secure the future of your practice is simple, but not easy. The right partner can make a big difference. Many of our clients ask me why Medicus chose to specialize in health care. The answer is quite simple: many of our family members are health care providers and we see first-hand the frustrations with technology that should actually be making things easier, not more difficult. We focus on your technology, so you can focus on your patients.

Perhaps diving into this topic created more questions than answers at this point. If you need help, please do not hesitate to reach out to either myself or my team here at Medicus Technologies. You can book a complimentary strategy call with myself or my partner Tim Smoot by visiting wesupportdocs.com/bookcall. We would be happy to answer any questions you have about what you have read here, or about cybersecurity in general.

About the Author

Steve Schabacker is CEO and co-founder of Medicus Technologies Inc. a Managed IT services company providing support and cybersecurity services to health care practices. Steve brings to the table 25 years of experience in the IT industry holding many different positions over the years. His diversified experience allows him a unique perspective and the ability view problems in a holistic manner.

Steve's team at Medicus technologies take great pride in helping health care providers. They believe that by taking care of technology, they allow their clients to focus on their patients.

You can connect with Steve online at https://www.linkedin.com/in/steve-schabacker/ and connect with Medicus Technologies at https://www.facebook.com/medicustech/ or www.medicustech.us.

Stealing Your Data, the New Old Fashioned Way

By Richard Avery

Imagine that you get up and slip into the office—it's a normal day like any other. You log onto your computer but you can't seem to log in to some of the websites you usually do and you can't get to some of the services that you want to access. Worse, other people in the office start to complain that they're experiencing the same thing. No one seems to understand what is going on; it's not just the websites for business that are inaccessible but personal ones, too. Everyone seems to be hit in some way, shape, or form. Bank accounts have wire transfers out, new credit lines have opened and are maxed out, even things like social media accounts have been taken over and altered. It isn't ransomware that has crippled you, but your business systems are as messed up as your personal life.

To take a break, you walk out of the office in frustration and find out that the company renting across the hall from yours has experienced some activity also, the same things happening to them as in your office. The security tapes from the night before show nothing, the firewall logs show nothing, the server shows nothing.

There is no trace of the issue because *I* broke into your office *five months ago* and have been living on your network ever since. I decided that last night was the time to pull the trigger and make use of everything I've got.

"Who are you?" you ask.

The OSI Layer

In the networking world, there is something called the open systems interconnection (OSI) layer. It has seven layers of communication, the first being the physical layer. Your cables and plugs, the unmanaged switches and network cards in your computers—these comprise the physical layer, but few managed service providers (MSPs) are helping clients manage physical security these days. Let's deconstruct what happened at the start of this chapter—how with a tiny amount of cost and some human psychology, a very low-skilled burglar can combine physical and logical penetration to wreak havoc on a business.

I, the aforementioned hacker, first can use compliance and policy guidelines against a business: I start with the physical doors to a business or building; ADA (Americans with

Disabilities) compliant door locks can, unfortunately, become a weak security point. For $50, I can get my hands on an under-the-door hook kit and use it to bypass the doors. With a little bit of training, I can get under or over the door in about a minute. Now I have access to your building. Unless there is an alarm system to deter me immediately, it's just a field day. Next, I move to the systems that I want to access, get data from, or dwell on. I unplug the computers or boot to a USB key if the computers are off. Maybe I need to type a few things in to boot to the key—maybe you have a BIOS password to slow me down. Depending on the model, I might have the backdoor passwords so those only slow me down a little bit.

If the computer is already turned on, I use a device called a "rubber ducky" that the computer thinks is a USB keyboard. It will load up the keyboard drivers and then "type" what I want it to do; that is, dump all your logged, saved passwords from all your browsers: Firefox, Chrome, Internet Explorer. These passwords might be encrypted but I really don't care, I also copy the hash out and other specifics that get technical, allowing me to log in as you into your business network. Typically, this process will work for all the desktops, and perhaps even the server room, as the latter is probably accessed by another ADA compliant door that I can easily bypass. Maybe I don't even care if the alarm goes off—the typical police response time is twenty minutes and I only need two or three minutes with a workstation.

I have my USB device scan for files called "accounts" or "passwords" or "stuff," anything I want, really. Maybe I have a while and can copy the whole server share if its small enough; the access isn't set up right so anyone can see it. Then it's just a matter of waiting. With all the data I retrieved from the business, I can set up some scripts and I can log into everyone's bank accounts, money transfer accounts, online auction accounts, or other avenues through which I can funnel and channel money.

I've waited 4-6 months since my physical break-in and my actual attack because any video recording system will have overwritten itself in that time, voiding any evidence of my presence. Unless there was an event, like an alarm trigger that night, no one is going to go back and look at the recordings. Small to medium businesses usually don't store that much surveillance back data.

Space Planning for Safety

Every business should ask themselves, "Is there a lockable door in front of our servers or can anyone walk in and pop in a USB as they walk by? Can the cleaning crew get access to everything so that all it takes is just one technical, under-the-radar employee who can steal all our information? Will our lack of security put us in a place where we have to report a breach?"

Windows should also be a primary concern when planning the layout of an office's workspaces and placement of equipment. We are at the point where technology is moving forward at such a huge pace that all I'd need to do as a data thief is invest in a good, $1000 camera with a 3000mm lens and an 80x + digital zoom. I could then steal data right off your screen through a window. With a good tripod and stabilizer, I can record a worker's full day of work and everything they touch. The laws I might be breaking, in fact, get very questionable and curious at this point.

My company had a client who had their business' entire backups stolen off their external drive. Here's what happened: the drive was in clear reach and view of a window. Someone threw a rock and less than thirty seconds later, the company lost their drive and all their data. Even though it was a backup and not their primary data storage, the data was not encrypted and the company had to report it as a breach. One might consider this a simple act of basic physical security, but the entire company was put at risk.

A solution for windows is polarized/solar film or security film. Solar film will help create a bit of a barrier for visibility into the building with the added bonus of reducing energy costs. Security film will create a huge deterrent for people trying to break in. Even with a hammer and proper tools, they will have a more difficult time, the attacker might not want to take the chance against time if you have window breaks tied into your security alarm system. They will most likely leave empty handed, without ever getting into your space.

The bottom line, when space planning, is that everyone needs to consider that physical access trumps everything else. Most non-IT people are unaware that even if you have passwords on devices, experts can bypass or reset physical and logical security using special commands or tools.

Preventative Protocols

The businesses more prone to a physical attack are smaller CPA offices, financial advisors, and bookkeepers—companies that have treasure troves of financial account data but typically don't have a decent security system in place or proper, preventative IT measures. How does a business keep something like this from happening? Let's go through a few pieces of information to help deter an attack like this, making the process frustrating—if not, impossible—for criminals.

1. **A single camera that is motion-activated, goes to the cloud, and is tied into an alarm system.** With a surveillance system like this, you can have something to look at when the alarm goes off. Even if the camera is covered or flash-lighted/lasered out, you have proof that an event happened for insurance purposes.

2. **Your office doors need to have a good floor "threshold strip."** This makes the space between the door and floor as thin as possible. If you can fit a key through that space, it's too big. There are tools that let criminals open deadbolts and activate push-bar doors utilizing the gap under the door. All of the door gaps into and within your office need to be thin, not just the doors with the ADA compliant handles. In addition, install the ADA compliant handles facing down or up so that its harder to hook them with the tools that are out there.

3. **Use BIOS passwords and hard drive passwords**. These can slow down the attack process and make it more frustrating. Unless the thief has some higher-level skill, getting in will be harder for them or at least deter them entirely.

4. **Turn off USB ports, put USB locks in place, or have management and monitoring of USB devices installed.** Maybe you have the front ports turned off so the person breaking in needs to spend more time trying. As a result, they might start questioning their tools or what other security they might run into.

5. **Encrypt your drives, even in your workstations**. Typically, this is something done for laptops or mobile devices, but there can sometimes be a hole in policy for the

implementation of this for desktops. A cyberthief can plug in their tools and immediately tell that they are dealing with encrypted drives that are unreadable. Once they get to this point, they might abandon their attempt because the amount of work and risk doesn't equal the payout.

A Thief's Investment Costs

At the lower end, a data thief's total investment cost for all tools they'd need for a physical attack is $100. If they wanted to splurge and get the things needed for breaking into a substantial number of businesses, the cost would increase to about $350. Either way, not a huge investment for a potentially high payload.

Half a year ago, we onboarded a new, local client and they had a rather complicated network. Their current IT company was massively overcharging them for very little service and a long list of gross incompetence that even went into the realm of possible legal liabilities. We called the IT company and asked them for the equipment passwords as no one onsite had them. In fact, none of the client's employees had received any documentation of their own IT situation. The client's network was a large one, with over 18 access points, 35 systems—all mobile, over 40 cameras, and 2 WiFi point-to-points that covered large areas of a ranch that supplied internet for two houses on the property. Worse still, this was a HIPAA client, so the lack of documentation was something for which they could be fined, hence the legal liabilities. All of the networking equipment was installed in a central rack that was in an attic, locked with an older Master Lock® brand, 175 model combination lock.

When I asked for the passwords, the IT company refused, saying they would not give them to me and that the point of contact was someone not onsite, someone who would most likely also not co-operate. While on the phone, I told them what I was going to do, that I was already past the Master Lock® device and, in fact, had already changed the combination. (There is a tool that lets you bypass the entire locking mechanism and just make it "pop open" so you can change the combination.) Then, I described how I was going to then take over the firewall/router; after that, the Wifi system, and how piece-by-piece I was going to remove their access. The resistance to help quickly fell away and I was passed on to a manager. By this point, I already had a cable plugged in and was about to bypass the device, so when a manager got on the phone, we had a short conversation and they agreed to provide me with access to everything. In just a few hours, we had the company's entire network locked down and systems changed. It was updated with new locks and reports were generated about the changes needed to make the company compliant moving forward.

Remember, your real risks and threats may not be coming from the faceless cyber world but may be physical invasions of your business. A thief may walk in through the front door or break a window, intruding into your technology space with hands to carry away valuable data and everything you care about.

About the Author

Richard Avery has been building computers and networks since the early 1990s. He also has in-depth experience and knowledge about physical security—since childhood he was trained by his locksmith father how physical and logical targets can be compromised and exploited. With seven CompTIA and 12 Microsoft certifications, as well as a list of others achievements, he went on to get a Bachelors in Network Administration. He then achieved an MBA in Marketing and an MBA in Management, as well as multiple executive certifications in Business Administration from

Notre Dame. He is also a Certified Cyber Security Analyst.

His career has taken him from small marketing companies across America to large technical firms. He spent a decade in the government military complex with jobs at Lockheed Martin and L3, including three deployments to Iraq and nine to Afghanistan as a military contractor. He focuses on combining physical security penetration with his logical hacking skill set to come up with the best and most cost-effective ways to protect his customers. He currently runs an IT consulting company called Titanium Computing in Austin, Texas, helping business owners navigate the complicated IT and security situations of today's age.

What to Look For in an Outsourced IT Security Firm

By Daryl D'Souza

If someone asked you what you should look for in a security system for your home, you might answer that installing a deadbolt would be adequate. But once you learned the statistics about how many homes are broken into—perhaps statistics for your own neighborhood—the level of security you need might become significantly greater. Add to that the possibility of family members being killed during a burglary and you might find yourself wanting the very best security available to protect your loved ones.

The same is true, or should be true, about securing your company's data. You won't understand what to look for in an IT company without understanding what risks exist today, where they come from, and why securing your data is so important. At Logicaal, we offer cybersecurity-first IT services for businesses of any size, from entrepreneurs to start-ups, small or medium businesses, charities, and non-profits. We are experts in data protection.

Why Securing Your Data Is Paramount

Your data is so crucial, it is almost the very essence of your company. If you don't believe that, you only have to look at companies who were forced out of business because of data breaches. Code Spaces is just one of the 60% of businesses forced to close their doors within six months of a cyberattack. In 2014, Code Spaces not only lost critical components of their data, but the attacker also deleted the company's backups, crippling the company and leaving it unable to function. In order to take stock of the risks, think about what would happen to your company if you suddenly lost—or lost access to—all of your data, including your back-ups. If this scenario would incapacitate your business, then you need to make the security of your data your number one priority.

What Cyber Attackers Want With Your Data

Data such as social security numbers and credit card information are obvious targets because of their value on the dark web. The dark web is a remote part of the internet out of reach of search engines, where criminals can conduct illegal activities. Think of it as the black market of the internet. Information that can have value on the dark web includes the aforementioned personal information, as well as email addresses, phone numbers, names and addresses. These are sold between cyber villains for nefarious purposes. In these cases, your data is copied and then stolen, but you may not even be aware that it has happened. Cybercriminals may also be after your cryptocurrency which they mine right out of your hard drive.

If your database doesn't include sensitive information like social security or credit card numbers, you may feel that your data needs less protection. But not all hackers are looking for that type of information. One piece of data that has the highest value to hackers is your credentials, or login information. Imagine if a thief could plant a device in your home that could detect the passcode to your security system as well as the combination to your safe. They could not only easily steal the belongings inside your house, but they could also change security credentials like your alarm code, effectively locking you out of your own house. Now just think about this happening to your business... you would no longer be able to access your computers or security system. Welcome to ransomware.

How Ransomware Can Destroy Your Business

Ransomware has been around for over thirty years but has become more sophisticated and more damaging of late. Ransomware can prohibit access to your data simply by changing your credentials, which is exactly what happened to Code Spaces. But an even more menacing aspect of ransomware is when it encrypts your data, making it nearly impossible to recover without the encryption key. In this case, your credentials still give you access to your data, but your data is useless to you because it is encrypted. With ransomware, the impetus is not the value your data has to the hacker, but what value your data has to you. In essence, the attacker is only concerned with what you would be willing to pay to save your business. What would you be willing to pay to regain control of your data and keep your business from destruction?

How Cyber Threats Enter Your System

Most people know to avoid certain sites or avoid opening emails with questionable attachments. Therefore, cybercriminals often concoct clever schemes and try to trick employees and business owners into providing the information needed for accessing their systems. Emails posing as official Apple, Paypal, or Google can, ironically, claim that the recipient needs to change their password because their account has been hacked. This is called "phishing," or "spear-phishing" if they are targeting a particular individual in a company. This is the type of attack that led DNC Chief, John Podesta, to give hackers his login information, in turn enabling them to hack the DNC network during the 2016 US presidential election.

If you or one of your employees has fallen for a phishing scheme, the effects may not be so obvious or public. For example, if a virus merely accesses a workstation, it can implant a keylogger, which quietly and secretly tracks and records keystrokes. One set of those keystrokes might be the login to your security system or database.

Another insidious type of attack is called social engineering. Social engineering involves using charm, persuasion, and maybe even a recording of a crying baby playing in the background to gain access to information that an unsuspecting customer service representative might not normally divulge. Some successful social engineering attacks involve multiple phone calls to different representatives, in order to gain valuable pieces of information during each call. Each piece of information can then be used on the next call to gain credibility. An attacker can call your cell phone provider, gain access to your cell phone account through social engineering, and then do a SIM swap. A SIM swap causes your phone number to move from your device to the SIM card on the hacker's device, which enables the thief to access all of your apps and private information as well as complete any two-factor authentication. This is all accomplished because an unsuspecting customer service representative bent the rules out of pity, trying to be helpful to someone they thought was a distraught customer.

Another threat that can bypass normal security measures is called a backdoor. A backdoor takes advantage of a weakness in the software to gain access to the system. This allows the attacker, unseen and undetected, to access computer files or infect the system with malware, trojans, worms, and other forms of cyber threats.

Why Traditional Anti-Virus Software Isn't Enough

Vaccines work by exposing the immune system to harmless subunits of a virus or bacteria so the body can develop antibodies that can fight the full, dangerous versions. Immunity to one virus does not lead to immunity to other viruses. Traditional computer anti-virus software operates in a similar way and with the same limitations. You have to know about and identify the code signature of a threat for anti-virus software to be effective in containing it. Identifying one virus or malware does not protect you from another. There are 350,000 new malware strains identified every day.

Security threats are becoming more highly developed and many can remain hidden from anti-virus software. Some malware can even intercept messages intended for your anti-virus software with a code version of a Jedi mind trick: the anti-virus software receives a false message that there are "no threats detected." Another type of threat that is successful in circumventing security software is file-less malware, which is a type of zero-footprint attack that does not install in the system but uses legitimate applications or even the operating system to invade a network.

Now that you understand the risks, you can better understand why the following things are important steps that an outsourced IT security firm should help you put into place.

1. Cybersecurity Education And Training

As you can see, the best anti-virus software in the world can't stop an attack if someone at your company doesn't recognize a phishing email. Not only should your employees have comprehensive training, but the training should be tested. An experienced IT security firm can recognize vulnerabilities that you and your staff would never consider. One area that is crucial to training is to ensure that employees understand that the use of their own devices is the greatest security threat to the company. An IT security firm will oversee policies and procedures for your staff to follow that govern passwords, internet usage at work, file storage on the server, updating of mobile devices, and any other activity that can affect the company's security.

2. Endpoint Detection and Response (EDR)

Since traditional anti-virus software is incapable of preventing the most crippling types of security threats, you can't rely on them alone to protect your business. Security threats will only get more sophisticated and more difficult to prevent. Rather than scanning for known viruses and needing constant updating, EDR checks a computer's vital signs to detect if a possible health problem exists.

An EDR can detect unusual CPU usage or abnormal application activity without needing to identify the virus or malware causing the problem. You should look for an IT firm that recommends EDR on all of your staff's notebooks, laptops, workstations, and desktops as well as your company's servers, storage, and network devices.

3. Proactive Security Measures and Critical Monitoring

Because of the sheer number and types of security threats that are constantly increasing, your company needs more than just a firewall at your network perimeter. Proper cybersecurity should involve an offensive or proactive approach rather than waiting for an obvious sign that there has been a breach. Some malware can sit in your system for quite a while gathering data before it causes a noticeable problem. A capable IT security firm should be hunting round-the-clock for security anomalies within your infrastructure, whether your data is on-premise, in the cloud, or a hybrid. You should also expect patch and AV updates, routine network maintenance, SPAM control, email archiving and continuity, as well as workstation and server auditing. Keeping your data safe requires constant monitoring to ensure that all of your software and workstations are up-to-date.

4. Immediate Quarantine when a Breach is Detected

When a security breach is identified, you want an experienced team of cybersecurity professionals ready to take immediate action. They should locate, quarantine, and disable the threat as well as identify intrusion points. Immediate response is crucial to ensure the protection of your data and infrastructure. If you attempt to handle a breach on your own, your amateur response can cause malware to begin deleting files, causing irreparable damage. Since many breaches come from phishing, drive-by downloads, and social engineering, additional staff training will likely be needed after a breach.

5. Business Continuity Plan

In this age of accelerated and continually advancing security challenges, it is not a matter of if your company will experience a security threat, but when. If the damage from a breach is significant, you need a plan in place that covers how you will continue operating your business. Any unnecessary downtime you experience can cost your company potential revenue that you can't afford to lose. You should expect an IT firm to work with you to create a business continuity plan. This plan will help prepare your business for returning to normal operations as soon as possible after a significant security attack.

6. Back-Ups and Disaster Recovery Plan

Most companies understand the importance of having a backup of their data, but where you store your backup is just as important as whether you have one. In the case of Code Spaces, the backup was accessible to the attacker and deleted, along with many essential files. Your backup should be out-of-reach of any security threats. Your IT firm should be backing up your data off-site, testing the data frequently, probing it for security threats, and notifying you immediately if there is a backup failure.

Why It Matters

Many companies only rely on their anti-virus software, firewall, and in-house IT department to keep their data safe. This may have been adequate in the past, but our new cyber reality is that determined cybercriminals can find a way around virtually any defense system you erect. The security landscape has changed dramatically just in the last year. You may think your business is too small to be a target, but the truth is that 58% of malware attacks are on small businesses, while 92% of malware attacks come from email. This means that you and your staff are the most vulnerable points in your current security system. This is why staff training is so important. They should not only be trained, but the effectiveness of their training should be tested to ensure they can recognize phishing emails.

If you have an in-house IT department that checks for security threats, this is a good start. However, your in-house IT team may only have training in routine IT responsibilities, not advanced protection from sophisticated cybercriminals. You are an expert in your field; you should find an expert in the business of data protection to keep your data safe. You would want a heart surgeon to perform a critical operation to save your life, not a general practitioner. You want an expert with experience, advanced tools, and specialized training, not someone with offhand knowledge. If your IT professional knows about plumbing, you would still call in a plumber if there were a broken pipe. The same should be true when it comes to enlisting specialized help to secure your data from cyber threats.

The most important reason to find a capable, qualified IT security firm to handle your security is so that you can focus on your business. You want peace of mind that all of the blood, sweat, and tears you've put into building your business won't be taken away because of a ransomware attack or major data breach.

Your business is worth whatever you need to do to protect it. Don't wait until you are left having to decide what you are willing to pay as a ransom to save your business. Spend your time focusing on building your business, not worrying about security threats. Leave that to the professionals.

Contact us at Logicaal to discuss your company's security risks at www.logicaal.com/contact.

References:

https://www.csoonline.com/article/2365062/code-spaces-forced-to-close-its-doors-after-security-incident.html

https://www.inc.com/joe-galvin/60-percent-of-small-businesses-fold-within-6-months-of-a-cyber-attack-heres-how-to-protect-yourself.html

https://spanning.com/blog/identity-theft-on-the-dark-web/

https://resources.infosecinstitute.com/a-brief-summary-of-encryption-method-used-in-widespread-ransomware/#gref

https://nakedsecurity.sophos.com/2016/12/16/dnc-chief-podesta-led-to-phishing-link-thanks-to-a-typo/https://www.techopedia.com/definition/4000/keylogger

https://www.consumer.ftc.gov/blog/2019/10/sim-swap-scams-how-protect-yourself

https://info.phishlabs.com/blog/sim-swap-attacks-two-factor-authentication-obsolete

https://blog.trendmicro.com/backdoor-attacks-work-protect/

https://resources.infosecinstitute.com/hardware-attacks-backdoors-and-electronic-component-qualification/#gref

https://www.av-test.org/en/statistics/malware/

https://www.csoonline.com/article/3227046/what-is-a-fileless-attack-how-hackers-invade-systems-without-installing-software.html

https://www.forbes.com/sites/ivywalker/2019/01/31/cybercriminals-have-your-business-their-crosshairs-and-your-employees-are-in-cahoots-with-them/#5f626cb41953

https://www.information-management.com/opinion/the-8-scariest-cybercrime-tricks-of-2019

About the Author

Daryl D'Souza is the founder of logicaal, a leading Cybersecurity-First information technology (IT) services firm that helps small and medium businesses protect their most critical asset: data. CompleTech from logicaal is an all-inclusive service encompassing all elements of an IT organization: the people, process and technology. CompleTech's key customers are businesses that are heavily reliant on technology regardless of their IT environment (on-premise, hybrid or cloud).

The security landscape has changed significantly and continues to evolve at a rapid pace. As the founder of logicaal, Daryl's goal is to ensure CompleTech, a pro-active risk monitoring, threat hunting and remediation service, is consistently aligned with today's evolving cybersecurity landscape, to ensure its customers can recover in a controlled and predictable manner when a cyber-attack occurs. Part of his responsibilities in this role includes developing new service offerings and working with product teams, service delivery, marketing and sales to ensure flawless execution.

Daryl brings a proven track record in information technology and professional services. Before devoting his work fulltime to logicaal, Daryl served as Director, Enterprise Solutions and later Managing Partner at Intrellis, a Global Managed IT Services firm whose clients include UNIQLO Canada, Assante Capital Management, Caffe Demetres, New Signature, Airtron Canada, Stratford Festival, Anxiety Disorder Association of Manitoba, Scotiabank Convention Centre (Niagara Falls) and Canadian Canola Growers Association. Prior to Intrellis, Daryl was part of the Advanced Solutions Group at Dell Canada where he assisted medium and large enterprises in designing efficient IT solutions that aligned with their business objectives.

A Business Continuity and Data Recovery Plan Helps You Weather the Storms

By Mike Bloomfield

In 2012, Superstorm Sandy ravaged the Upper East Coast, especially the coasts of Staten Island, New York. New York Governor, Andrew Cuomo, estimated that the damage caused by Sandy was $33 billion, and nearly 38,000 people on Staten Island were without power the day after the storm. The storm undoubtably caused Staten Island-based businesses to lose equipment and data, whether from flooding, fires, or power outages. For some businesses, the damage was too much to overcome and they had to close their doors.

Superstorm Sandy will always be a painful reminder of what can happen to a business if its IT infrastructure isn't properly protected with a business continuity and data recovery (BC/DR) plan. Although a storm of Sandy's magnitude hasn't hit Staten Island since 2012, there have been other threats that have developed in the intervening eight years. Ransomware made global news in 2017 when the WannaCry strain infected over 230,000 computers in more than 150 countries.[12] Only a month later, the Petya strain devasted Ukraine especially, plus 80 companies located in Russia, Germany, the United States, and more.[13] While ransomware was certainly not new to the scene, these attacks were some of the first to make major global headlines.

Disasters, whether natural or unnatural, do not discriminate. They will strike no matter where you are located or what time of the year. This is why it is of vital importance to engage the services of a managed services provider (MSP)—but not all MSPs are created equal. So what does our company, Tekie Geek, do that makes us so unique? The Geeks stress complete BC/DR as a top priority for nearly every SMB we manage.

A Tekie Geek BC/DR plan ensures that no matter the time or cause, a business can continue to operate as if nothing happened. Datto, Tekie Geek's BC/DR partner, ensures that a business's

---

[12] https://www.washingtonpost.com/world/national-security/us-set-to-declare-north-korea-carried-out-massive-wannacry-cyber-attack/2017/12/18/509deb1c-e446-11e7-a65d-1ac0fd7f097e_story.html

[13] https://www.dw.com/en/wave-of-new-cyberattacks-spreads-hitting-multinationals/a-39444187

valuable data is protected, and, if disaster does strike, that business is recovered in as little time as possible. Datto has products and tools that allow the business owner (and the Tekie Geeks techs) to sleep soundly at night knowing that data is properly protected from all angles of attack. Any true BC/DR solution will allow instant virtualization of the server from both the local appliance or from the cloud. Why both? If a server crashes, virtualization from the local appliance allows for quicker recovery and data synchronization than from the cloud. The Datto device can act as a temporary server while the client orders a new one or replaces the broken components.

After a flood destroyed a number of servers at a Tekie Geek client's business, a Datto device was used in a temporary role. The device worked so well that it took weeks of convincing the client to order new servers! If the device was destroyed in this situation, then Datto would have shipped a new device overnight, with the client's data preinstalled.

RTO and RPO Assessments

Tekie Geek's emphasis is on keeping the client's recovery time objective (RTO) and recovery point objective (RPO) as low as possible. RTO is the amount of time it takes to get all services running like normal after a disaster event. RTO starts the second an attack happens, not when the tech team or the business notices there's been an attack. When planning the RTO for a business, Tekie Geek considers three points: how much downtime can this business afford, their budget, and what is the exact plan after an attack commences.

RPO focuses on the data side of recovery. It outlines how much data a business is willing to lose from a disaster. Most businesses have their own definitions or measurements regarding which data is worth backing up and how often these backups should happen. Once an hour, day, week, month—no two businesses are the same. With Datto, however, backups can occur as frequently as every fifteen minutes. When working with verticals such as medical or design, this frequency isn't overkill—it's critical. How much time and effort would be lost if an architecture company lost a day or week of work because a ransomware attack hit them before a backup could occur? With Datto backups, it doesn't matter when a disaster strikes. If ransomware infects a server, the RTO can be as little as five minutes. According to Datto's "2019 Global State of the Channel Report," one in five small businesses (SMBs) have experienced a ransomware attack in the last year; half of those reported experiencing business-threatening downtime. Tekie Geek understands that when the risks are this high, only a high-end backup solution is sufficient.

While Tekie Geek and Datto have saved a number of clients from disasters, it certainly isn't prudent to have only a BC/DR in place. The holes in an infrastructure need to be plugged so that a recovery isn't happening every week. In order to fully protect a business from disaster, Tekie Geek implements a number of products and solutions to mitigate the chance of a disaster. When walking through solutions with a prospective client, the first recommendation is a security assessment. When you're sick, you don't just walk into a pharmacy and demand medication. You need to first see a doctor who will give you a proper diagnosis and prescription. The same can be applied to an SMB and its network. Tekie Geek will always recommend starting with a security assessment, which is a total evaluation of an SMB's workstations, servers, network, backups, and anything else connected to the internet. Tekie Geek's software will scan for unprotected personally identifiable information (PII), unsafe end user behaviors, uninstalled OS and software updates, and more. When completed, a consolidated and full report is generated covering both the network and security. In order to fully understand how crucial this process is, you need to know that the end user is always the biggest weakness in every business. Therefore, it is critical to cover any entry point a hacker could use to get to that end user.

A number of tools can fulfill this purpose. A spam email filter is a good start, as 66% of MSPs report that phishing emails are the top ransomware delivery method (Datto's "2019 Global State of the

Channel Report"). Should any malicious emails find their way through the filter, then its important that end users are properly trained to identify such threats. Since a hacker only needs to be right once, every employee and boss needs to complete and understand the cyber security training they receive, whether in person with Tekie Geek or through online seminars. Proper password policies and protection is a part of training the staff. It's frighteningly common how basic password rules are ignored or unknown to those outside the IT community. End users need to understand that writing passwords down on sticky notes, sharing passwords, and storing passwords in Excel is reckless and endangers a business. Implementing a password management tool alleviates these concerns. Multi-factor authentication, or MFA, can protect workstations and software while end users are away from their desks. Should an outside actor attempt to log in to a workstation with a stolen password, then there is no way to proceed. A notification is sent to the end user's phone asking to verify the log-in (which hopefully will be declined).

The cybercrime business is booming. Bitdefender stated in 2017 that ransomware payments exceeded $2 billion.[14] As the number of criminals who develop and spread ransomware increases every year, the MSPs who defend their clients need

---

[14] https://www.cyberscoop.com/ransomware-2-billion-bitdefender-gpu-encryption/

to be experts in their field. The one-man shop that only does break-fix is no longer sufficient for protection against modern threats. The MSPs that don't emphasize BC/DR and cybersecurity will eventually bite the dust. We saw this in 2019— hackers were breaching MSPs and pushing ransomware through successfully. Not only does this essentially kill any chance of a business recovering, it also creates a bad name for the MSPs that are doing their jobs the best they can.

Tekie Geek practices what we preach. Everything we recommend to our clients we have implemented in our office. We use MFA for all log-ins, we use Datto backups, we even fake phish our own staff to keep them on their toes! The criminals only need to be right once, but we have to be right every time. Only extreme vigilance ensures that SMBs will be protected from the worst-case scenario.

When I look back over the last seven years, I'm proud of the staff I've assembled and the work we've done. Client retention is 99% and we aim to keep it that way as long as possible. We recently moved into larger office space. We're quickly outgrowing where we started! The future is bright with Tekie Geek as we continue to expand into the new decade.

About the Author

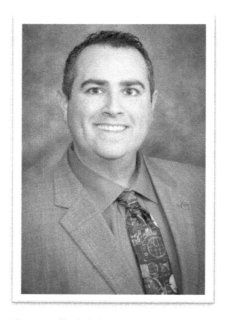

When Mike Bloomfield founded Tekie Geek in 2013, he came from an extensive background in business and technology. He was the Manager of Product Engineering for six years at American Traffic Solutions. If you've ever been ticketed for speeding or running a red light anywhere in the United States, there is a good chance that Mike's team designed the software running on that camera. In addition, for six years, Mike was the Director of Research and Development/IT at Apple Industries, Inc., one of the largest photobooth companies in the world. However, after over a decade of commuting, Mike desired to work closer to his family and help people more directly. Like most managed service providers, Tekie Geek started as a one-man shop. In its seven years of business, it has grown to eight full-time employees managing thousands of workstations and dozens of small-to-medium sized business across New York City, New Jersey, Long Island, and upstate New York.

https://www.tekiegeek.com/

Phone: 347-830-7322

Cybersecurity for Nonprofits

By Steve Haviland

At their hearts, nonprofits are about service above self. Nonprofits have a mission—they contribute to our local communities in profound and fulfilling ways. Nonprofits are humble, providing services without rewards or big profits. The revenue that is generated goes back out to pay staff and to create programs and projects that benefit the whole community.

So, your nonprofit is not a target for criminals, right? After all, you don't have a million-dollar bank account, you don't drive a Tesla, and your goals are altruistic.

Unfortunately, you couldn't be more wrong. Lack of investment in technology, a mix of volunteer and paid staff, inconsistent policies, large databases full of information about both clients and donors, and many more factors make nonprofits an irresistible target for cyber criminals.

Catastrophic Effects

When criminals steal information from nonprofits, the consequences can be devastating, not only to the nonprofits involved but also to our most vulnerable community members. For instance, a food bank may have to freeze programs while it recovers from a cyber crime. With its programs frozen, families in the community go hungry.

Nonprofits can lose their ability to receive donations, or worse yet, be blacklisted by donors, foundation partners, corporate sponsors, and government institutions. These consequences are catastrophic and can affect any size of organization.

To see these consequences in action, one needs to look no further than the story of a local pet shelter as reported by *Wired* in December, 2018.[15]

"As the founder and director of a nonprofit animal shelter on the East Coast, Alana has spent most of the past decade caring for pets that might otherwise be euthanized. Her work also resonates with people online—the Facebook page for the shelter has more than 1.3 million followers. But in August, she noticed something strange: A series of unfamiliar posts began appearing on the page, and no one at the shelter could say where they were

---

[15] https://www.wired.com/story/nonprofits-facebook-get-hacked-need-help/

coming from. For several days, Alana and her staff simply deleted them. It didn't initially occur to Alana that her account may have been breached."

The article proceeds to recount the details of the cyberattack:

"Then, in the early morning hours of August 19, a link to a fraudulent GoFundMe fund-raiser appeared on the shelter's page, claiming the nonprofit was raising money for pets displaced by wildfires thousands of miles away in California. By the time Alana spotted the fund-raiser, it had already raised around $1,500. She quickly crafted a Facebook post alerting donors that it was fake, but it was useless. "The post was immediately removed," says Alana, who for privacy reasons requested that her last name and the name of the shelter not be used.

Another staff member soon discovered that a stranger had been added as an administrator to the shelter's Facebook page nearly two months earlier, silently waiting for the right opportunity to act. In a Facebook Messenger chat, the stranger warned the animal shelter to stop telling people the fund-raiser was bogus. "If I see one more post we will delete the page forever," he wrote.

Frightened and angry, Alana scrambled to ensure GoFundMe canceled the fund-raiser, which it did. "Our fraud protection measures prevented this individual from gaining access to any of the funds raised. This user has been banned and the money has been refunded to donors," a spokesperson for GoFundMe said in a statement.

But the incident marked only the beginning of what would become a months-long struggle between Alana and a hacker determined to steal her nonprofit's donations—by weaponizing Facebook."

The catastrophic effects of a cyber attack, like the one targeting Alana, not only harm some of our most at-risk populations, they also damage a nonprofit's reputation and credibility. Nonprofits seem to be at a crossroads, mandated to use new technologies to stay relevant in their mission and with their donors, yet exposed because of a lack of funding to properly protect themselves.

The Barriers to Entry for Nonprofit Cyber-security

There is an alarming gap between the current state of readiness that nonprofit organizations have with regard to cybersecurity, and best practice. It is a threat to the entire sector, to donors, grant-makers, essential programs and services, and to those who use nonprofit services.

Yet, there is cause for hope, because of a growing consensus that nonprofit cybersecurity is a serious issue. There are low cost, yet significant and powerful tools, procedures, and practices that can be leveraged to ensure cybersafety for nonprofits and the communities they serve. So why aren't we seeing more progress? What are the roadblocks and contributing factors that make cybersecurity so hard for nonprofit organizations?

The number one issue recognized by the nonprofit community is lack of funding for cybersecurity initiatives. Many foundations see technology funding as something that should be considered part of overhead, thus outside of their funding guidelines. Meanwhile, organizations with limited resources face a choice between providing their services or allocating funds to improve their cybersecurity. Leaders must make a choice about where to put their resources and the large majority of non-grant donations continue to go towards delivering services.

Complicating the issue of funding is a huge problem with executive buy-in. Nonprofit boards and leaders do not feel that cybersecurity is a danger that they need to take seriously, despite great evidence to the contrary. Cybersecurity initiatives fail when they do not have executive sponsorship and a clear mandate from the board.

Two final factors round out the top barriers to improving cybersecurity in a meaningful way. First is a general lack of knowledge about technology in the nonprofit sector. Nonprofit leaders, while truly gifted at accomplishing organizational missions, widely lack general knowledge about information technology, much less the specialized knowledge required to implement strong cybersecurity practices. Second, weak infrastructure—due to inadequate investment and implementation—compounds the problem.

These barriers to implementing proper cybersecurity practices are interwoven and difficult to overcome. However, there are some things that the educated, nonprofit leader can do to turn these things around.

Building Awareness For Nonprofit Leaders

We live in a world that is truly awash with information. In a few clicks of the mouse, I can learn about George Washington, the moon landing, or my favorite television series. Never has information been so available, and never has it been so easy to monetize that information. Entire digital ecosystems and marketplaces have grown up around our desire to share information. No one would argue that websites like Facebook, Google, and Twitter have been developed and designed to monetize the information that other people have. Likewise, you would receive few arguments that criminals monetize information through phishing, ransomware, malware, and other techniques. Why then are nonprofit leaders so reluctant to consider this threat legitimate?

Every day, we are surrounded by headlines about how another large organization got hacked, and how more of our sensitive information is in the hands of the bad guys. However, we only ever hear about the big guys, and we relax in the false confidence that our organizations are too insignificant to matter. The truth, of course, is that cybercriminals steal millions of dollars every day from tens of thousands of organizations. We don't hear about these attacks, because often times, they go unreported.

Under-reporting of cybercrime is, of course, a symptom of a more complex problem. Consider that in the cybersecurity community, significant praise and accolades are given to the individuals who discover new ways to hack computer systems. However, if you are one of the organizations affected by such security issues, the picture isn't as rosy. Your organization can appear weak, ill-prepared, greedy, lazy, or worse yet, ignorant. As a leader, you can appear incompetent and foolish for not taking cybersecurity seriously. There is huge incentive to hide that your organization has been hacked.

It's understandable that those leaders who have not yet been impacted can treat the risk with such a cavalier, devil-may-care attitude. This requires a cultural change, and the best way to deliver that to the nonprofit community is through capacity-building grants.

For non-profit organizations, capacity-building grants such as those funding professional development of staff, strategic planning, assessments, or board development can also be used to provide cybersecurity education and develop critical knowledge that creates a culture of security. Concurrently, nonprofits have access to low cost, affordable, and commonsense training, cybersecurity tools, strategy, and processes that leaders can use to build security-aware boards, staff, and services. A great resource for this type of training is the website Keep My Nonprofit Safe, www.keep mynonprofitsafe.com.

The human element of the cybersecurity equation—that is, building awareness and caution—cannot be overlooked. Powerful cybersecurity training for staff, leadership, and board members is perhaps the least expensive, most impactful item in which a nonprofit can invest.

When properly executed, training like this should encapsulate a multi-hour "at-your-own-pace" online training component, monthly 2-3 minute training sessions accompanied by quizzes, simulated phishing campaigns, and management reporting. A program like this is a powerful approach that will build awareness among leadership and caution among staff. The end result—a nonprofit organization that is less likely to become the victim of a cybercrime.

Investing in Nonprofit Cybersecurity

Funding is the single biggest limiting factor in the nonprofit world and nonprofit leaders face three distinct decisions when it comes to investing in cybersecurity:

1. They can pay for cybersecurity services out of their general funds.

2. They can ignore cybersecurity funding, focusing instead on their mission.

3. They can build cybersecurity funding into their grant requests.

In today's environment, options one and two seem the most popular choices.

Paying Out of General Funds

Direct funding grants for cybersecurity efforts are rare. Largely, you do not find dollars set aside for cybersecurity as part of infrastructure upgrade grants, and when you do, oftentimes the funder includes advice and directives that constrain the way that funds can be spent. The results are often cybersecurity infrastructures that do not align with or fit the nonprofit organization's unique needs and requirements.

Organizations who self-fund must commit to capital and operational expenses over multi-year terms. This is difficult, considering that annual funding cycles do not always generate consistent revenue. As a result, self-funded organizations will sometimes cut cybersecurity expenses when finances become constricted and when the organization is at its most vulnerable.

Ignoring Cybersecurity Entirely

Of course, choosing to ignore cybersecurity completely is the worst option, because these organizations become irresistible targets for cyber criminals. The nonprofit, its donors, and clients become critically vulnerable to cybersecurity threats. These organizations may also find themselves out of compliance with state and federal laws, making them criminally negligent.

Funding Through Grants

For organizations who are going to seek funding from grants, the terrain can be challenging. Donors and grant makers want to see a positive change—a real community impact—from the dollars they invest. This raises an interesting, chicken-and-egg problem: how can donors, foundations, and other grant makers expect their funds to make a real community impact if those dollars are stolen by cyber criminals?

How Fund Providers Can Encourage Cybersecurity

Foundations and other grant makers are starting to develop an understanding of the two main classes of information that cyber criminals seek: personally identifiable information (PII) and personal health information (PHI). Nonprofit organizations maintain donor records as well as records for our most vulnerable communities, and because of this, are valuable targets for criminal enterprise. Foundations and other grant makers are starting to see that investments in cybersecurity are required; what remains to be seen is how they will structure funding for such initiatives.

What we currently know is that most foundations and grant makers consider funding for cybersecurity and technology as overhead cost and not part of delivering programs. This model is failing because nonprofit organizations do not always have the overhead funds necessary to invest properly in cybersecurity initiatives.

Instead, foundations and other funders should consider cybersecurity as an essential part of program delivery. They can encourage nonprofits to value their cybersecurity by asking grant applicants to include cybersecurity as a priority line item in their budgets and logic models.

With a relatively small investment—either as a grant pool for existing grantees or as an additional funding amount for existing grants—foundations and other grant makers can create a positive impact on the nonprofit cybersecurity landscape.

Consider how the world might change if funding organizations expected grant applications to include the cost of technologically safeguarding a program as part of its cost.

A New Standard for Nonprofit Cybersecurity

I imagine a future in which all nonprofits have exceptional cybersecurity programs in place while still providing the services and programs that make such profound differences in our communities. In order to accomplish this goal, the nonprofit sector must adopt a new standard of cybersecurity that will empower organizations through its funding models, provide training, promote executive buy-in, and provide clear guidelines of what "good" cybersecurity looks like.

All of this starts with the funding paradigm of grant makers and foundations. The program officers and directors of these organizations need to understand and maintain current knowledge about cybersecurity standards. This will enable them to identify concerns when reviewing grant applications around exposure to PII and PHI, and allow them to ask additional questions about data protection and cybersecurity. A great idea is to invite a technology or cybersecurity professional to take part in the grant review process or sit on the committee.

Another missing piece of the puzzle is cybersecurity training and access to security consulting services as part of a capacity-building program. The knowledge resources at www.keepmynonprof itsafe.com are world class and can help nonprofit leaders build awareness in their organizations about the need for cybersecurity. Sharing knowledge resources like KeepMyNonprofitSafe to everyone in the nonprofit sector is critical to success. These types of resources are well-positioned to provide detailed training from the grant program officer level all the way down to the non-profit staff level.

Finally, engaging in meaningful conversations and removing the stigma around cybersecurity breaches is one of the most critical pieces to success. Nonprofit organizations must be able to openly share without repercussions about how they were breached, in order to promote awareness. Technical resources should be able to share information to make sure that what effects one nonprofit does not become an enterprise that can impact them all.

All nonprofit organizations have to make a decision about how they spend resources on cybersecurity and information security. As we have become technology dependent, the threats have changed and cybercrime has become inevitable. The only question that remains for nonprofits is: Will you pay now for good cybersecurity, or pay later when you are attempting to recover from a breach?

About the Author

Steve Haviland is a leader who knows how to read a balance sheet, an engineer who knows how to configure a firewall, a loving father, and a raving sci-fi fan, in that order. Steve Haviland is the CEO and Founder of Think of IT Computer Services. With 20 years of experience in corporate information technology, Steve is equally at home in the board room or working on complex technology challenges.

Steve is a passionate advocate for the effective use of information technology in the nonprofit space and in giving back to his community. As a community member for the Nonprofit Technology

Enterprise Network and the chair of the Keep My Nonprofit Safe IT Provider Alliance he has authored many papers on the effective us of technology for nonprofits.   Steve is a member of the Southwest Rotary Club of Wichita Falls where he endeavors to give back to his local community by serving as the Service Projects Chair for his rotary club.

Visit Keep My Nonprofit Safe, www.keepmynonprofitsafe.com.

The Methods and Madness of Social Engineering

By Blake Haigler

The responsibilities of a business owner have drastically changed over the years. Whether you are in your very first year as an entrepreneur or have been running your business for many years, the chances are high that you have encountered many changes throughout the years. For my business, providing IT services to other companies, I have seen dramatic change from 2005 when I acquired my first client providing Network Security, Firewall Management, and General Monitoring Services. Technology and people have both changed, requiring many business owners to adapt and change the way they do business.

While having my IT company has been challenging, rewarding, time consuming, and fun at times, I would not change it for the world. Along the way, I have made some mistakes and I have also had some big successes that have made me the business owner that I am today. Luckily, I have also been able to change "with the times" and create a company culture that is flexible and open to change. A few things that have changed over the years of conducting business are communication methods, working remotely versus going into an office, improved technology, and social engineering. The last item is the term used to describe the tactics cybercriminals use to exploit your business network and gain access to your confidential data. They manipulate or deceive victims through human psychology; they exploit human vulnerabilities in order to gain access to computer systems and business networks, buildings, confidential data, and much more.

Manipulating people through social engineering has been a part of our world for decades, dating all the way back to the Trojan War. The ancient Greeks built a wooden horse as a supposed gift but hid soldiers inside, deceiving the Trojans into opening their gates. This allowed the Greeks to infiltrate the Trojans unknowingly. This same tactic is used today by hackers with modern technology.

As an IT professional, social engineering is one of the most significant changes I have noticed throughout the years. In this chapter, I am going to explain how social engineering will affect your business in 2020 and how you can get in front of the hacking and protect your business from cybercrime. If you believe that hacking is not a serious concern, you only have to open a newspaper or turn on the news to see that it is a real issue in our world today.

Hackers may use methods to access your business computer and/or networks using phones, email, direct mail or direct contact with their intended victims. The most common methods of hacking today are phishing, spear phishing, smishing, vishing, and CEO fraud. Most of these are attempts made by hackers to trick victims into providing personal information, credentials, access to business workstations and ultimately, their network. Hackers are getting smarter and using more advanced methods to try to trick their victims. This includes fake emails with links in them that look like they are from someone you know, as well as fake texts and phone calls.

Have you ever received a telephone call from someone asking you to confirm your information before the caller tells you what they are calling about? How about a recent call saying they are from the IRS telling you that you owe money to the government? These are very popular "vishing" attempts by hackers who are getting good at tricking or manipulating their victims into giving them what they want. In the case of the increasingly popular IRS vishing scams, the caller pretends they are from the IRS and indicates that they have an important message regarding your taxes. The caller proceeds to indicate that the victim owes $X amount and is requested to make payment as soon as possible. The caller provides the victim with the information for where to send their payment. If the victim sends the requested money, they end up sending money to a hacker, NOT to the IRS. Consequently, the victim will never see their money or hear from that caller ever again.

In 2019, you probably saw the influx of fake emails that were sent to you and your employees. How many of your employees clicked on the links? It's scary to think that your business network could have a virus that was unknowingly loaded and is lying dormant in your system, ready to ruin your day/week/month, or even year. Many companies around the world have viruses lying dormant on their systems, waiting to deploy at the right moment.

Kevin Mitnick, a world-renowned hacker, once stated:

> *"The key to **social engineering** is influencing a person to do something that allows the hacker to gain access to information or your network....To some people, I'll always be the bad guy.... What I found personally to be true was that it's easier to manipulate people rather than technology."*

This being the case, hackers have turned their attention to using mischievous methods on individuals instead of directly utilizing technology. Technology is now only a sub-tool, not the primary tool. Manipulation of people has become a quicker and more profitable way for hackers, forcing security professionals to continually adapt to more up-to-date techniques for defense.

Why is the issue of cybercrime so vast? Well, the criminals don't stop and they are constantly evolving. As time progresses, so do changes in technology and advancements in cyber warfare. These days, hackers are extremely intelligent and can be anyone (your neighbor, the kid bagging your groceries, the barista pouring your coffee); there are zero stereotypes about what a hacker looks like or from where they come. Cybercrime is even more concerning because there is almost little to nothing we can do to **prevent** hackers from finding your information and taking it to use for anything they want if you don't put specific protections in place.

A hacker is no longer a kid in his mom's basement making a joke out of the misfortune of others. People have created criminal empires—with call centers, telemarketers, managers, and everything else that comes with the structure of a business. Hackers are making millions—and the amount is expected to be in the billions—in 2020. These numbers are supported in many research articles performed by highly reputable companies like *Forbes*, IBM, and *Statista*.

Cybercrime is getting worse and hackers are finding new ways to manipulate technology to get what they want out of their victims. Protecting your biggest assets has become one of the most important tasks for business owners this century. So, what can be done to stop hackers?

How to Secure Your Business Against Cybercrime

There are a few things that you can do *right now* to help protect your business from social engineering, including: cyber security awareness training, email security, multifactor authentication, advanced endpoint protection, firewalls, and so much more.

Cyber Security Awareness Training

Employees are the number one threat to businesses world-wide. This means that more than likely, one of your employees will be the cause of a cyber breach. The fact of the matter is, unless you are standing right behind each employee every time they open an email, access an unfamiliar website or even download something from the internet, you cannot protect yourself from your employees 100% of the time. So, what can you do instead? Have your employees complete cyber security awareness training and create a cyber security conscious culture within your organization. It will only benefit your company if your employees are more aware of cybercrime and know what to do to prevent being victimized. Trust me, the cost of NOT conducting cyber security awareness training could be your entire business or livelihood.

Email Security

Another tool I suggest that all businesses put in place is email security. Email encryption, for example, will help protect confidential information such as a credit card number or social security number that is sent via email transmission. If your email is not encrypted or secure, hackers can gain access to data transmitted within your and your employees' emails and post it on the dark web for other criminals to exploit however they see fit. The idea behind email security is to protect you and your employees' email messages and attachments that are sent over untrusted networks outside of your organization. With email security, you will ensure that emails sent to and from your organization are secure. It is important that you are doing at least the very basic things to help protect your business against hackers. This is an excellent investment that you can make for your business.

Multifactor Authentication

Another critical tool that your business needs to have in place right now is multifactor authentication (also known as MFA or 2FA). Multifactor authentication is a security tool that requires your system(s) to authenticate logins using two different methods to confirm a user's identity for a login transaction. For example, in order to log in to your computer, you will need a password and then a 6-digit code from either your mobile device or online authenticator. You may have recently seen multifactor authentication for your Facebook account in which a personal identification number (PIN) is sent to your cell phone prior to letting you access your profile. This is an example of MFA.

Multifactor authentication has become the single most effective access control management tool that helps businesses protect themselves from cyberattacks. When MFA is implemented properly, this security can protect against hackers accessing your network if credentials become compromised. How many times have you or your employees lost their laptops or mobile devices and you knew there was company data maintained on either of those devices? With MFA enabled, third parties would not be able to access the system or mobile device without that second authentication (PIN code). Multifactor authentication should be implemented throughout your organization in order to protect your assets.

Advanced Endpoint Protection

What if I told you that antivirus software was dead and is completely useless against hackers? I know that sounds harsh, but it's true. The antivirus we knew back in the early 2000s is pretty much dead and has been replaced by what is known as Advanced Endpoint Protection (AEP) security solutions. In IT terminology an "endpoint" refers to the end user or the person for which the software program or hardware device is designed, like laptops, tablets, and mobile devices.

Due to the sophistication of technology and the vast number of digital tools at our fingertips, antivirus is considered obsolete. The tools we use have evolved to more "advanced" methods with the ability to secure endpoints against known and unknown attacks. AEP is especially beneficial for those employees that you have working remotely as AEP will secure each remote workstation/laptop in order to secure your business network by blocking access attempts. AEP really is a win-win and something your business needs to put in place today in order to stay protected.

Firewalls

Another tool your business should have in place, if you don't already, is a firewall. Firewalls help block unauthorized access to your business network while allowing you and your employees the ability to securely transmit data from the network or internet. Essentially, firewalls are simply a hardware or software device that filters the information that is transmitted to and from the internet. Firewalls can be implemented within your business in a number of ways, depending on the size of your business and your business needs. It is absolutely imperative that your business has a firewall to help protect your private business network and all of your private and business assets.

I could write an entire book on the many tools you can utilize to help protect your business from hackers. The bottom line is, social engineering and human hacking have become an epidemic and will continue to ruin businesses in 2020. I have seen businesses crumble after being hit by just one cyberattack. The opportunity cost of neglecting your cyber security to protect your business is far less than the risk of closing your doors after being hit by ransomware.

You have probably heard the news and seen many articles about cybercrime effecting all types of businesses: small to large, government, privately owned, public—it does not matter the business type because hackers do not discriminate! They do not see size, company type, demographics or anything of that nature. You know what they see? Your IP address and the shiny new object which is your business network. Do not wait until it is too late to realize that social engineering and human hacking is a reality and will only get worse in 2020. Take steps to protect your business.

About the Author

Born in 1982, as a small skinny kid with very little muscle mass, Blake Haigler was raised with the constant sense of security and safety. In his early years as a child, he trained in martial arts. As he got older, he wanted to help train others and went on to become an instructor. Unknowingly, this started Blake on a path of learning about people and the way to communicate, altering how they view things in a different way.

Blake moved on to join the US Marines, furthering his ability to assist and protect people. In the Marines, Blake learned even more about communicating with people and multiple ways to achieve goals. After the military, his education was a priority and because of his passion for protecting people and his interest in the cyber world, it only made sense to become an expert in cyber security.

Blake has dedicated his entire life to security and keeping people safe. Currently holding multiple licenses concerning security, with the ability to extract information from a simple conversation, he has built a company to assist and train mid-level and enterprise level staff on security processes and safety measures within this new world of constant evolving threats. To learn these secrets, reach out to Blake via phone (704) 298-1414 or visit Social.Haiglersystems.com.

Ransomware, Phishing and Vishing: How To Prepare Your SMB

By Chris Wanamaker

The security landscape today isn't what it was a few years ago. As systems and networks continue to become more complex, as we digitize more personal information, and as we continue to integrate different types of devices such as internet of things (IoT) and cloud and mobile assets, the avenues available for hackers to attack is only increasing.

For IT security professionals, it's a cat-and-mouse game. We're working to keep the bad guys out at the same time they're looking for new ways to get in. We're constantly educating ourselves on the newest threats, latest prevention technology, and most recent tightening of governmental security compliance regulations. It takes a full-time staff just to research the threats, dissect the compliance regulations, and implement the best security strategies to keep a business and its important information safe.

Regardless of your business size or the industry of which you're a part, you *ARE* a target. The notion of "I'm too small of a business" or "I don't have information the hackers want" is not applicable in today's growing world of cyber threats. Last year alone, ransomware generated over $25 million in revenue.[16] Will your business be the next one paying a ransom to get your own data back?

In this chapter, we're going to look at the different methods hackers use to compromise your business information, how their activities affect your viability, and what you can do to protect yourself.

What Is Ransomware, Phishing and Vishing?

Ransomware

Ransomware is one of the most frequently-used terms and which most people are familiar—it's been happening with greater frequency in recent years. In 2019, global enterprise ransomware attacks happened more than 440,000 times. That's equivalent to one new company falling victim to an attack every 14 seconds. It's estimated that by the

---

[16] https://spinbackup.com/blog/24-biggest-ransomware-attacks-in-2019/

year 2021, it will become one company every 11 seconds.[17]

Ransomware, by definition, is a type of malicious software designed to block access to a computer system until a sum of money is paid to the hacker. Over the last few years, there have been numerous stories in the news about healthcare organizations, schools and universities, and state and municipal governments being shut down because of a ransomware attack. When your files are encrypted and you're unable to access them, it's impossible to continue with "business as usual."

Phishing

Another common, but not as frequently used of a term, is "phishing." You may have heard it referred to as "CEO fraud" or even "spoofing." Regardless, phishing is the practice of sending fraudulent emails purporting to be from reputable companies. These emails are sent in order to induce individuals to reveal personal information such as passwords, social security numbers, and credit card information.

In nearly 91% of recent cyberattacks and data breaches, phishing was the top cause.[18] This is attributed to several factors, including the availability of targetable information as well as an increase in the sophistication of the emails being

---

[17] Ibid.

[18] https://digitalguardian.com/blog/91-percent-cyber-attacks-start-phishing-email-heres-how-protect-against-phishing

sent. In 2019, over 76% of businesses[19] had reported they were the victim of a phishing attack.

Vishing

Vishing, short for "voice phishing," is one of the least common terms you'll hear, and one of the more difficult ones to protect yourself against. Similar to phishing, vishing is the practice of making fraudulent phone calls or leaving voice messages. These calls purport to be from reputable companies, in order to induce individuals to reveal personal information such as bank details or credit card numbers.

Common forms of vishing are the types of calls informing you that your vehicle's warranty is about to expire, there are lower interest rates available for your credit card, or you've won an all-expenses paid stay at a name-brand hotel. While these calls were designed to get information from consumers, the bad guys have adapted these techniques to go after businesses, who have far more potential than consumers. Their fraudulent calls might ask you to try accessing a new payroll website or request that you update your credit card information to avoid having your internet services disconnected.

---

[19] https://blog.dashlane.com/phishing-statistics/

Why All of This Matters: Some Facts To Consider

- Ransomware attacks have increased over 97% in the last two years[20], and there is no sign they'll be slowing down anytime soon

- All businesses are targets because your information is important to you and preventing access to it is profitable for hackers

- Phishing emails, one of the top causes of recent data breaches, has increased 109% over the last year alone[21] and the emails are getting highly sophisticated

- Governmental agencies are tightening security standards and increasing penalties for businesses who fail to comply

- 1 in 5 businesses who experience a ransomware attack never re-open their doors to customers[22]

- 73% of businesses do not feel like they are adequately prepared for an attack or data breach.[23]

---

[20] https://www.smbhd.com/ransomware-in-iot/
[21] https://purplesec.us/resources/cyber-security-statistics/
[22] https://www.computerweekly.com/news/450301845/One-in-five-businesses-hit-by-ransomware-are-forced-to-close-study-shows
[23] https://blog.tbconsulting.com/tbconsulting-73-of-companies-are-unprepared-for-a-cybersecurity-attack-is-yours

The Cost and Destruction Caused by Ransomware and Data Breaches

While there are hundreds of ransomware and data breach examples available online (and probably many more that never go public), the following ones are the most powerful examples of why you should be concerned and take action now to protect your business from becoming the next headline.

- City of Baltimore, Maryland

A ransomware strain known as "RobbinHood" encrypted several critical functions for the city of Baltimore in May 2019. The swath of damage included the total malfunctioning of voice systems, email systems and online payment portals. A ransom of $76,000 was requested by the hackers but was not paid as the city endeavored to restore the infected systems and data on their own. As a result, the city lost over $8 million in revenue and expects to pay over $10 million in the recovery effort which includes data analysis, new hardware, and new software.

- The Heritage Company

Just days before Christmas 2019, this Arkansas-based company sent home more than 300 employees and told them to find new jobs after IT recovery efforts from a ransomware attack two months earlier failed. Company representatives said "hundreds of thousands of dollars" were lost because of the incident and it would be nearly impossible for the company to continue operating as it had before.[24]

- City of New Orleans, Louisiana

In December 2019, a city employee clicked a phishing email and provided their credentials to hackers which led to a large volume of additional phishing emails being sent to the city's systems. Within a few days of the attack, the City of New Orleans had incurred nearly $1 million in costs, presumably due to the cost of lost revenue, system replacements, ransomware payments, employee downtime and forensics.[25]

- Campbell County Health

Hackers breached this community health system and locked up sensitive patient information and medical devices. In the days after the attack, the health system was forced to cancel services; their cash registers, email and fax systems were unavailable, and doctors had to resort to pen and paper to document medical conditions. Further, they had no access to prescription records which forced patients to bring their medication bottles with them to visits.[26]

- Demant

---

[24] https://www.zdnet.com/article/company-shuts-down-because-of-ransomware-leaves-300-without-jobs-just-before-holidays/
[25] https://www.nola.com/news/politics/article_8dbed526-37d0-11ea-9998-bbe9bfc93b5b.html
[26] https://www.fiercehealthcare.com/tech/campbell-county-health-wyoming-hit-ransomware-attack-diverts-er-patients

This hearing aid manufacturer took the top spot for estimated losses occurring from a ransomware attack in 2019. The data breach, estimated to have cost the company upwards of $95 million, shut down the organization's enterprise resource planning (ERP) system, production and distribution facilities in Poland, and production and service sites in Mexico, among others. The global reach of this attack took the company weeks to begin recovering from, costing them lost sales and increasing production delays.[27]

Why Not Protecting Your Business Is Irresponsible

As an employer, you're responsible for protecting your customers' information and your employees' livelihood. If you're operating a business and you don't have a security-first mindset, you're putting it all at risk. The cost and destruction caused by ransomware and data breaches is just one piece of a much larger and more complex puzzle.

Federal and state governments have been enacting legislation to protect customer privacy and outline standards for data protection and IT security. The long list of compliance regulations include the Health Insurance Portability and Accountability Act (HIPAA), the Health Information Technology For Economic and Clinical Health (HITECH) Act, the California Consumer Privacy Act

---

[27] https://www.zdnet.com/article/ransomware-incident-to-cost-danish-company-a-whopping-95-million/

(CCPA), the New York SHIELD Act, the National Institute of Standards and Technology (NIST) Cyber Security Framework, and the Cyber Security Maturity Model Certification (CMMC).

Do you know to which of these laws you're legally required to abide by? Do you know what the penalties are for not complying? How are you tracking updates and changes to these laws or frameworks?

Not only can the cost from ransomware payments, system downtime, or lost sales cause your business financial stress, but the fines and fees from failed compliance will potentially force you to close your doors for good.

How To Prepare Your SMB From Going Out of Business

As a business owner, you're passionate about your industry and how your business helps its customers. You know how to do that well. But do you know how to protect the complex technology setups on which your company relies? Do you know how to educate your staff on increasing their security awareness? Are you continually testing and evaluating your risk exposure?

In order to prepare your SMB from going out of business due to a ransomware attack, phishing campaign or data breach, here are a few things I recommend you do.

- Change Your Security Mindset

Security is no longer just a firewall on your network or antivirus software on your computer. Proper security is like an onion—multiple, connected layers. Additionally, you'll want to move towards a Zero Trust environment and technology that utilizes advanced Artificial Intelligence to protect you.

- Develop and Implement Company-wide Policies

Protecting your business information starts with how your employees conduct themselves on the company's network and assets. Defining acceptable internet usage and advanced security policies help limit what employees have access to. Additionally, developing a breach response and disaster recovery plan will ensure your response to an attack is swift—minimizing the impact to your business.

- Thoroughly Educate, Consistently Test, and Reinforce Principles

Teaching your employees how to spot a phishing email or recognize a data breach starts with thoroughly educating them on the current threat landscape. However, you must consistently test their comprehension of this knowledge. Additionally, reinforcing a culture of "see something, say something" will allow employees to feel empowered to report unusual activity instead of ignore it.

- Continually Assess Your Risk

Even the slightest change on a network can open up your business to a potential attack. As a responsible business owner, you'll want to continually assess your potential risk against new threats and changes in legislation.

- Partner with a Trusted Managed Services Provider

Managed Services Providers specialize in knowing where to start and help keep your business in compliance. They will start with a thorough cybersecurity audit of your infrastructure and provide recommendations on the best ways to protect your business from becoming another headline on the evening news.

About the Author

Chris Wanamaker, a 20-year veteran of the IT industry, is the Co-Founder and CEO of Business Technology Services, headquartered in Phoenix, Arizona. Also known as GeeksHD, his business, a Managed Services company, offers a range of security and managed technology solutions to business clients who range in size from 10 to 500 employees.

Chris began his career serving the consumer market as a consultant and, using the knowledge he gained, formed his first Managed Services company in the mid 2000s. Chris' laser-targeted focus on securing systems and networks is coupled with his desire to educate clients on the threat landscape and how to protect themselves. This was the driving force behind his continued growth.

Today, Chris works with business owners to help them navigate the complex security landscape. He helps business owners better understand their compliance requirements, develop security-first mindsets through policies, provides training programs, and manages security solutions. Chris' passion is building solutions to problems others couldn't solve and improving efficiencies in complex environments. His belief is that true partnerships are built on the results of actions and making every interaction a win-win situation.

For more information on the security and managed technology solutions he provides, to schedule a no-cost 30-minute meeting with Chris, or to see what your current Business Risk Score is, visit https://www.geekshd.com/hackproofbook.

CEO Fraud is Everyone's Concern

By Jerry W. Swartz

What is CEO Fraud?

CEO fraud is a popular scam in which cybercriminals spoof company email accounts and/or text messages, or place static-plagued phone calls to impersonate high-level executives. Then they will try to use social engineering to fool an employee—such as an executive administrator, someone in accounting, or HR—into executing unauthorized wire transfers, or to reply with sensitive information.

CEO fraud, also referred to as Business Email Compromise (BEC), is a type of email attack that relies on the art of deception that uses a more advanced form of sophistication than traditional phishing attacks. Hackers using BEC do careful research in order to use specific knowledge for impersonating a company executive, trusted brand, or partner.

- 91% of breaches start with email[28]
- 96% of business received some sort of BEC during the second half of 201729

According to the FBI, Between June 2016 and July 2019, BEC campaigns caused just over $8.3 billion in actual and attempted losses around the world, including $3.5 billion in the US30. BEC uses a variety of deception techniques such as:

- Display name deception
- Domain spoofing
- Lookalike domains
- Social engineering
- Fake phone calls and text messages

An attacker hacks into a corporate email account and impersonates the business' real owner to defraud the company, its partners, customers, and/or employees into sending sensitive data or money to the hacker's account.

How It Works:

- The scam starts with research: The attacker will sift through publicly available information about a company from their website, press releases, and even social media posts.

---

[28] Social engineering, in the context of cyber security, is the psychological manipulation of people to perform actions or divulge confidential information.
[29] https://blog.infogressive.com/business-email-compromise
[30] https://www.ic3.gov/media/2019/190910.aspx#fn2

- They learn where a company is located, the names of the executives, and other organizations with which a company works.

- They will learn everything they can about a company's employees and even spouses, children and pets from social media sites such as LinkedIn, Facebook, or Twitter.

- Once they learn a company's structure, fraudsters begin to research and target specific people within the organization based on their specific goals. If they are looking for money, they may target the Accounting department and accounts payable personnel. If they want access to data and servers, they might target the IT department personnel, if they want tax information—HR, customer data and financials— they'll target accounts receivables.

- They look for the names and official titles of company executives, the corporate hierarchy, and they even know executives' travel plans from email auto replies which state exactly how long the person will be out of the office.

- They then will attempt to gain access to an executive's email account. To remain undetected, they might use rules or change the reply-to address so the executive will not be alerted when the scam is executed.

- Another trick is to create an email with a spoofed domain, which, if not scrutinized, may fool an employee into downloading a malicious link and opening up their company email to the hacker's control.

- After completing their research of a company and scouting the corporate communications for some time, the hacker has insight into how their scam might work. They will have a good idea of who is responsible for wire transfers and might then create a scenario requiring the immediate transfer of funds. If a company has many suppliers, the hackers might also create fake invoices to accounting for the rush payment of materials.

- Once they determine what they want and who they will target, they begin to build their attack. The hacker most likely will craft some sort of spear phishing campaign at this point in hopes of infiltrating the company. Unlike traditional phishing campaigns, spear phishing campaigns are custom emails targeting a very select group of people. These emails are extremely realistic looking and very hard to detect. They often appear to come from someone within the company or someone with which the company does business. These emails may contain the same jargon coworkers use, they may include such things as company logos and even the signature of an executive.

Some red flags to watch out for include:

- Illegitimate email addresses: If not scrutinized, these can lead to a malicious download.

- A sense of urgency evoked in the communication: The purpose of these emails is to create a sense of urgency and demand the recipient take immediate action without checking with others. Remember, the hacker's goal here is to rush the receiver into making a mistake, one that may cost them their job and cost the company a lot of money.

- An unexpected request: If the email is asking to verify or update something that the recipient didn't recently update or if the email is a sudden, strange request for financial transfers or valuable personal information from a boss, it is very likely that a hack is in progress. Due diligence is required and remember to verify any request with the requesting party before financial or sensitive information is sent.

- Incorrect email signature.

- Email sent to a personal account.

- Lookalike domains and display names: Watch out for hyphens, dashes, and periods where they don't belong. Always look closely at the domain name.

BEC: Targeting the Most Vulnerable

While a BEC scam can target anyone in a company, it will typically aim for the high-level executives and people working in the finance department. Also known as "whaling" and/or the aforementioned "CEO fraud," this type of scam is significantly more difficult to detect than traditional phishing scams because it is so targeted. Education is key when it comes to spotting malicious emails. Every single employee is susceptible to phishing emails and it only takes one click or one person responding to potentially cause a breach. Phishing and security training of all employees periodically throughout the year is a must.

6 Tips or Strategies to Solve this Problem

1. Ongoing and regular cyber training for all employees: Evaluate staff compliance with internal protocols by using real-world security awareness testing, performance updating, and reviews (fake phishing of all staff). This is a must for employers. The human element remains a hacker's greatest weapon, and as such, employees should be trained on identifying fraudulent emails.

2. Use an enterprise level SPAM filtering solution: This filters and tags external emails to help easily highlight spoofed accounts.

3. Confirm and verify email requests for fund transfers: Employees should be trained to verify these requests either in-person or with an immediate supervisor. In-person is best; if not, then by phone using an independently obtained phone number or one that you already have on file. Be on the lookout for transfers requested to new or recently updated accounts. Employees should be very skeptical of urgent and rush money transfer requests, especially coming from C-level executives.

4. Use dual control for all money movement activities: Policies should be put into place requiring that any transfer over a set amount be verified and signed off by both the employee and their respective supervisor. This allows for two levels of scrutiny and two sets of eyes to help prevent illegitimate fund transfers.

5. Use multifactor authentication for web-based email accounts: Multi-factor authentication should be implemented in order to prevent unauthorized access of emails and will help avoid fraudsters leveraging actual accounts of executives and/or employees through spear phishing campaigns.

6. Communicate quickly when fraud or breaches occur: Notify key banking partners and IT security staff immediately if you suspect a BEC. Contact law enforcement and file a complaint with the FBI Internet Crime Complaint Center. Also, check with state laws to see if they have a time period for notifying clients of a breach or loss of information.

Case Examples of BEC

Xoom Corporation: One real world BEC example is what happened to the Xoom Corporation, an online, international wire-transfer provider headquartered in California. Spoofed emails sent to their finance department resulted in multiple transfers totaling over $30.8 million to fake overseas accounts[31].

Operation WireWire: Earlier this year, the Department of Homeland Security, the Department of Treasury, and the US Postal Inspection Service arrested 74 people in the United States, Nigeria, Canada, Mauritius and Poland as part of Operation WireWire. As part of the takedown, federal law enforcement seized nearly $2.4 million and recovered $14 million in fraudulent wire transfers.[32]

---

[31] https://duo.com/decipher/that-email-is-not-from-the-ceo-its-a-bec-scam
[32] https://www.ic3.gov/media/2019/190910.aspx

Lithuanian Cybercriminal: This hacker used email addresses of suppliers and targeted companies such as Apple and Facebook. By impersonating suppliers, he was able to steal $100 million over two years.33

Chinese Hackers: According to the Economic Times, Chinese hackers stole $18.6 million from the Indian arm of Tecnimont SpA, an Italian engineering company, through an elaborate cyber fraud scheme impersonating the firm's chief executive. The scammers sent emails from an account that looked deceptively like the one used by the Italian group's CEO, as well as organized conference calls to discuss a "confidential" acquisition in China. These conference calls included people pretending to be the group's CEO, a top Switzerland-based lawyer, and other senior executives of the company. The hackers requested that the Indian branch head transfer money for an acquisition in China, convincing him that the money couldn't be transferred from Italy due to regulatory issues. The India head transferred the amount in three batches during November 2017 over a one-week period. Each transfer—$5.6 million, $9.4 million, and $3.6 million—was sent to banks in Hong Kong and withdrawn within minutes.[34]

---

[33] https://digitalguardian.com/blog/what-business-e-mail-compromise-how-it-works-best-practices-and-more

[34] https://www.bankinfosecurity.com/bec-scam-leads-to-theft-186-million-fraud-a-11930

These case studies illustrate real-world examples of how prevalent BEC is and how devastating it can be for a business. Be sure to implement the suggestions in this book so that you don't become a statistic.

About the Author

Jerry W. Swartz is the founder of Krypto IT Services LLC, a Cybersecurity & IT Consulting firm based in Houston, Texas. He is an experienced Chief Executive Officer with a demonstrated history of working in the information technology, security and service industries. Skilled in Customer Relationship Management (CRM), Data Center, Management, Software as a Service (SaaS), Outsourced Project Management and Networking Administration. Through his company, Krypto IT, he and his team of professionals provide a unique blend of scalable, remote IT & cloud-based solutions, resources, and skill sets to address today's threats and future Cybersecurity support needs of businesses & enterprises. He has been in the tech field since 1995 and has been contracted by companies such as United Airlines, EDS, Memorial Hermann, and Texaco to name a few. Our clients consist of Auto dealerships, Medical Practices, Law Firms, Manufacturers and businesses of all sizes. He is also a heart transplant survivor who goes to the local hospitals to give support and mentor patients who are waiting for transplant such as the left ventricle assist device, LVAD, recipients.

For a free offer for book purchasers, visit www.BookOffer.KryptoCyberSecurity.com.

Mastery of Layers

By Paul Mancuso

Vincent William Van Gogh was one of the most prolific artists among his contemporaries. He is credited with over 2100 artworks, including approximately 860 oil paintings in just over a decade of work. To this day, he is considered one of the greatest artists of all time. *Starry Night*, painted in 1889, is one of the most iconic and recognizable pieces of art ever created. The many layers of color and the expressive brush strokes pull you into the painting—even today, with all the technology we have, great appreciation is found in artworks such as this. What makes an artist great? What makes an architect innovative? What makes a chef sought-after? What makes you the best at what you do?

A celebrated artist has mastered color, technique, and an understanding of their subject. A top chef is not only good at one dish, but is skilled at combining flavors and textures to create an array of signature dishes. An accomplished architect brings in the right builders and team to create memorable, iconic structures. What do they all have in common? They have all mastered the use of layering all the necessary elements in their domain to achieve their greatest work.

Think about you in your business. Every business—no matter how big or small—has layers. You may have layers of people internally that work for you and help you execute your vision. You may have external professionals who handle your logistics or your legal matters. Or you may have many layers to the services you offer. In one way or another, the layers in your line of work are what sets you apart from your competition. Those layers make you an "artist."

The IT Layer

The most common layer, one that is often neglected in business, is information technology or "IT." You may have a friend or family member that is "good with computers" and they have handled your IT needs with no major issues. The difference in the world today is that the landscape of IT changes almost daily, and you need an expert in that field to make sure your IT infrastructure is reliable, and most importantly, secure. If you do not currently have an IT security expert as one of your business' foundational layers, you need to find one immediately. You would not draft legal documents without the advice of your attorney, so why would you make IT decisions without an IT expert's recommendations and guidance?

Not all IT experts are the same. Just like other experts, you must be very careful when choosing an IT company. Make sure they have your best interest in mind. Here are the top two things to look for when choosing an IT or managed services provider (MSP):

1. **Partner with the right people.** I cannot stress this enough; you really should consider finding an outside IT company with which to partner. You are not looking to hire a vendor or employee, but rather, a partner who will help bring value to your business and help you utilize technology for the enhancement and growth of your company. It is important that the company you choose is not just handling problems as they arise but also helps think through business processes as you grow, providing recommendations on technology improvements as necessary. You need an IT provider who looks out for you, not just collects checks from you as your IT issues happen or things break. Finding a company that is like-minded and is an expert in their field will pay dividends well into the future as you grow.

2. **Find a "Security First" IT company.** If the IT companies you are looking at do not start with security, you may want to keep looking. A security first company will ensure that your data and business is secure, thus ensuring a smooth-running business process for you. Since security in the IT industry changes so much, you want to be very careful about

making sure they are focused on security and staying up-to-date with current trends. They need to be thinking about the impact your business would suffer in the event of a data breach or ransomware attack. Also, be cautious of any company that claims they can stop all attacks or guarantees no breaches. In the IT industry today, you need to find a company that can help you come up with a controlled, reliable, and organized plan in the event of a breach or ransomware-type attack. You should have a very up-front conversation about how much downtime your business could potentially experience and how quickly they could get you back up and running.

Priorities. After you have decided on a company that is security first and is ready to partner with you, it is important that your basic needs will be looked after and prioritized. Your chosen IT company should come up with a well-rounded security plan for you, and I want to educate you on the top five areas that should be covered at a minimum. This is not an exhaustive list but the very basic minimum you need to address to ensure your security:

1. **Hardware**. Your first line of defense for protecting your network and business files is addressing your employee workstations and your router. You want to make sure all your workstations are current—with the most

recent operating system and security patches. Your business network is only as secure as your least secure workstation. All workstations and servers should also be secured with the latest in end-point protection services. Your main router should be an enterprise-grade router that is capable of remote security updates and intrusion protection. If you have multi-site in your business, you want to make sure you have a VPN capable router as well. This will secure all traffic and monitor incoming connections. Do not use consumer routers in a business environment.

2. **Server or Desktop Backups.** If you are a small enough company that you do not use a server, you want to make sure all your workstations are backed up automatically to a cloud provider. If you have a server, the same applies. Depending on the size of your business, you may also want to put a physical appliance in place for server backups in the event of a server failure. If your business relies on employees working remotely, you may want to invest and look into a cloud-based, enterprise-grade file sharing solution that has file versioning and sharing permissions as well.

3. **Email Backup and Security.** In 94% of all security breaches, email is the entry point.[35]

---

[35] Page 13 of Verizon 2019 Data Breach Investigations Report.

People assume that if email is cloud hosted, it is already secure from threats. As the security landscape continues to change, more and more users are experiencing breaches, and, in some cases, ransomware infects their cloud-based email accounts. You should consider an email security and backup plan for all email accounts related to your business. A good security package will have URL filtering as a feature that will check and scan any link in any email to verify if it is a known phishing site trying to steal your information. If it is, the filtering will block the user from accessing that site. Other features to look for are: SPAM filtering, email encryption, and email archiving. In addition to a security package, you also want to have a backup solution for your email. In addition to protecting you from accidental deletion or a rogue employee, a backup solution will ensure you have a backup of all your email files in the event your cloud account gets infected with ransomware.

4. **DNS Filtering.** A good layer of protection is to use a DNS filter for your end users. Simply explained, a DNS filter will block known malicious sites from accessing from your business network. An added benefit is the ability to block other sites such as gambling, adult websites, and other categories of your choosing. Many of these services also give you the ability to extend filtering to mobile

devices and laptops on any network, not just in the office. This helps keep devices secure no matter the physical location.

5. **Password Management.** Many users have very simple or easy-to-guess passwords. In fact, the number one password revealed in data breaches is 123456.[36] Again, I cannot stress enough how your entire security is only as strong as the weakest area. It might be a weak password, or it might be a computer that needs patching. One of the ways you can help your employees keep their passwords secure is to enlist a password management software for them to use. Many of these programs today will auto generate passwords and store them in an encrypted file, as well as give them the ability to share their passwords with other users securely. Enforcing good password management is one of the best, cheapest ways you can keep your data secure. Often, I have found that people choose convenience over security. Until they have a data breach, that is. Be proactive in your password management to make sure you keep your business secure. Make sure you are setting an example to your staff, modeling what good password management looks like and not coming up

---

[36] https://www.cnn.com/2019/04/22/uk/most-common-passwords-scli-gbr-intl/index.html

with ways to circumvent your own security guidelines.

Ludwig van Beethoven knew about layers. Think about the layers of sounds and musical notes in his music and the precision with which orchestras put it all together. Each instrument played individually and combined together makes for an extraordinary expression of Beethoven's music. Just as the individual layers are necessary for the masterpieces of Van Gogh and Beethoven, you must look at IT security as a requisite layer in your own business. Within the IT layer, there are also IT security layers all their own that you have to bundle together to secure your business. No one solution will make you secure and just one piece of software will not provide security for you. It must be a layered approach to provide a cybersecure foundation for your employees, workstations, and ultimately your business as a whole.

My father used to tell me all the time, "Measure twice and cut once." That statement transcends carpentry with a broader, important lesson: plan instead of react. In building, it's best to plan and measure an area twice before you cut it wrong and have to repair it. In the same way, it is best to have a security plan in place instead of hoping that a breach does not occur. Keeping your business secure is your responsibility—to your staff and yourself.

It has been said that the best way to ensure you spend more money on IT is to try spending less money on it upfront. Once your files become encrypted due to ransomware, many companies will pay whatever price is needed to recover their data. IT security is too important for you to try and manage on your own; you need to find a security expert who is ready to partner with you.

Is IT security one of your business' foundational layers? If the answer is "no," start this layer now!

About the Author

Paul Mancuso is the President and CEO of Vital Integrators based out of Lafayette, LA. Vital Integrators currently has 10 staff members and has customers along the Gulf Coast from Texas to Florida. Paul has a unique perspective and understanding of the IT industry as a Managed Service Provider but also installs and designs audio, video, and lighting systems for churches and businesses that have a strong desire to integrate those systems around a core IT infrastructure. He desires to provide a personal and accurate service to clients by helping both businesses and end users fully utilize technology to enhance day to day operations.

Paul excels in the field of network and systems integration, as well as managing corporate networks. He specializes in finding better, more efficient, and more creative ways of accomplishing goals, which frequently prove to be more cost-effective. He is extremely motivated by the challenge of helping to redirect the course of an organization through the proper use of technology, and he takes great satisfaction in helping them save money in the process. Paul resides in Lafayette, LA with his wife Misty and sons Landon and Greyson.

If you are interested in an IT assessment or need security consulting, schedule a meeting with Paul Mancuso by using the information below.

Website: www.vitalintegrators.com

Phone: 337.313.4200

Social Media: @vitalintegrators

Top 5 Cyber Safety Practice Tips for the Busy Therapist

By Amjad & Imtiaz Khanmohamed

When you are a health care provider, patients trust you with their Protected Health Information (PHI). Because a patient's PHI record contains personal information that identifies an individual and describes his or her health status, sex, age, ethnicity, or other demographic characteristics, it is a serious target for cybercriminals involved in identity theft.

According to Robert Lord of Bridgewater Associates, PHI and Electronic Health Records (EHR) contain all your patients' exploitable information. Today, it is the most comprehensive record of a person's identity. EHR records are worth hundreds and thousands of dollars on the dark web. According to research by *Forbes* magazine and *Twilio*, the going rate for a social security number is $0.10, whereas PHI records are worth $10.00. The health care industry ranks second behind the financial services industry as the most heavily cyber-attacked sector.

In addition to a patient's health records, a PHI also contains information such as intake forms, lab work requests, therapist's notes that refer to a patient by name, dictation tapes, telephone conversations with patients, encounter sheets, insurance claim forms, and e-mail messages. All of it is extremely sensitive personal information. And unlike financial information, health information is permanent. Credit cards and bank accounts can be changed but the PHI of your patients is forever.

Cyberthreats and the Dark Web

Cyber threats on the dark web are serious. *Investopedia.com* describes the dark web as: "… encrypted online content that is not indexed by conventional search engines. Also known as the 'darknet,' the dark web is a component of the deep web that describes the wider breadth of content that does not appear through regular internet browsing activities." Cybercriminals use the dark web to carry out their transactions, including the buying and selling of vital personal information.

Protection for Your Patients' PHI

Your patients' PHI records are in your transmitted and stored emails, your phones, iPads, tablets, DVDs, USB devices, computers, scheduling calendars, electronic faxes, billing and clinical practice management software, and other electronic tools you use. Because PHI records are subject to transmission over the internet, fortunately they are covered by the Health Insurance Portability and Accountability Act (HIPAA), Health Information Technology for Economic and Clinical Health (HITECH) Act, and other laws. These laws provide a compliance framework for clinical practitioners regarding their patients' PHI.

HIPAA and HITECH

In 1996, a significant piece of legislation commonly known as HIPAA—or the Health Insurance Portability and Accountability Act—was made into law. In 2009, President Barack Obama signed the Health Information Technology for Economic and Clinical Health Act (HITECH Act). HIPAA, HITECH, and subsequent laws recognize that all healthcare providers and related business are now using digital tools instead of paper records. These regulations exist to provide policies for safeguarding your patient files and procedures to follow in the event of a breach.

Here are **5 key areas** of HIPAA and HITECH:

1. Documentation
2. Business Associates
3. Privacy
4. Security
5. Breach

The scope of this chapter is to provide you with tools to implement the compliance requirements of HIPAA and HITECH. It is a basic overview, providing you with a framework to take action towards compliance. It is not comprehensive and does not address specific compliance elements that may apply to you.

Much of the information in this chapter is further explained in greater detail on the HIPAA Journal website. It is an excellent resource.

https://www.hipaajournal.com/hipaa-resources/

1. Documentation

A HIPAA document is more than a policy. It's proof you care about protecting your patient data.

A massive chunk of your HIPAA compliance process should be spent recording what you've completed. This step is known as **documentation**, and though considered a pain by many people, this process is necessary for HIPAA compliance.

Documentation helps others comprehend what has been done, what still needs to be done, and where the problems are in your environment. Documentation is the failsafe that keeps your hands clean, keeps your company transparent, and keeps your security efforts organized. HIPAA and HITECH compliant documentation should include the following:

- HIPAA Risk Management Plan
- HIPAA Risk Analysis
- PHI location documentation (e.g. a PHI map)

- Notice of Privacy Practices
- How you've eliminated third party risks
- Software development lifecycles
- Business Associate Agreements (BAA) and/or Enforceable Consent Agreements (ECA)
- How the environment is coping with identified vulnerabilities
- Incident response plan/breach response plan
- Current/future goals and milestones
- Explanation of unimplemented, addressable implementation standards
- Work desk procedures
- Training logs
- Compliant processes and procedures
- List of authorized wireless access points
- List of all devices including physical locations, serial numbers, and makes/models
- Electronic commerce agreements
- Trading partner security requirements
- Lists of vendors
- Lists of employees and their access to systems
- Diagram of your physical office, including exit locations
- Disaster recovery book

- Employee handbook
- Policies and procedures for the Security Rule, Privacy Rule, and Breach Notification Rule.

2. Business Associates

HITECH requires that a covered entity (a clinical practitioner or clinical organization) confirm that any written arrangements or contracts contain specific information regarding their Business Associate compliance. The contract must include:

- A description of the permitted and required uses of health information protected as part of HIPAA compliance
- Statements that the business associate will not disclose protected information other than what is required by law
- Proper safeguards to protect the information from material breach or violation as well as steps to take should a data breach occur.

In addition, a covered entity must have the right to terminate any agreement with a Business Associate should the data breach not be addressed. The covered entity must report any failure to address a security problem to the Department of Health and Human Services Office for Civil Rights.

3. Privacy

The Privacy standards address the use and disclosure of individuals' health information—their PHI—by the covered entities subject to the Privacy

Rule. It also addresses the standards for individuals' privacy rights so they understand and can control how their health information is used. Within HHS, the Office for Civil Rights (OCR) is responsible for implementing and enforcing the Privacy Rule with respect to voluntary compliance activities and civil money penalties.

A major goal of the Privacy Rule is to assure that individuals' health information is properly protected while allowing for the flow of health information that is needed for providing and promoting high quality health care. The Privacy Rule also exists to protect the public's health and well-being. The Rule strikes a balance that permits important uses of information, while protecting the privacy of people who seek care and healing. Given that the health care marketplace is diverse, the Privacy Rule is designed to be flexible and comprehensive, in order to cover the variety of uses and disclosures that require addressing.

4. Security

Prior to HIPAA, no generally-accepted set of security standards or general requirements for protecting health information existed in the health care industry. At the same time, new technologies were evolving, and the health care industry began to move away from paper processes and rely more heavily on the use of electronic information systems. Paying claims, answering eligibility questions, providing health information, and conducting a host of other administrative and clinically-based functions were increasingly digital.

Today, providers are using clinical applications such as computerized therapist order entry systems, electronic health records (EHR), and computerized radiology, pharmacy, and laboratory systems. Health plans are providing digital access to claims and care management, as well as member self-service applications. While this means that the medical workforce can be more mobile and efficient (i.e. therapists can check patient records and notes from wherever they are), the rise in the adoption rate of these technologies increases the potential security risks.

5. Breach

The HIPAA Breach Notification Rule requires covered entities to notify affected individuals, the Department of Health and Human Services (HHS), and in some cases, the media, of a breach in an unsecured PHI. Generally, a breach is an impermissible use or disclosure under the Privacy Rule that compromises the security or privacy of a person's PHI.

The impermissible use or disclosure of PHI is presumed to be a breach unless you demonstrate there is a low probability the PHI has been compromised based on a risk assessment of at least the following factors:

- The nature and extent of the PHI involved, including the types of identifiers and the likelihood of re-identification

- The unauthorized person who used the PHI or to whom the disclosure was made

- Whether the PHI was actually acquired or viewed

- The extent to which the risk to the PHI has been mitigated. Most notifications must be provided without unreasonable delay and no later than 60 days following the breach discovery.

Notifications of smaller breaches affecting fewer than 500 individuals may be submitted to HHS annually. The Breach Notification Rule also requires business associates of covered entities to notify the covered entity of breaches at or by the business associate.

HIPAA and HITECH are complex, and non-compliance carries huge risks to your practice's finances and reputation. There are daily cases of larger, far better-equipped hospitals and clinics to which fines have been levied and reputation damaged permanently as a result of failure to meet HIPAA and HITECH requirements. Our goal is to educate with an introductory guide which will help you understand a very complex law that affects you and your patients.

Compliance at your Clinic

Building A Culture of Privacy

Conversations at your clinic and throughout the office might be overheard. Patients in the reception area and staff might be discussing patient records, and staff responding to phone calls or scheduling appointments could be easily overheard. As a start, provide training to staff regarding privacy concerns, install privacy glass, and have conversations confidentially. Here are some specific suggestions for protecting patient privacy:

- Patient sign-in sheets should have minimal information and should be changed frequently. For example, these documents should not contain a visit's reason or purpose.

- Provide every patient with the Notice of Privacy Practices (NPP) Form and ensure they sign it to acknowledge they have received and understand it.

- Safeguard your work area: do not place notes with confidential information in places that are easy viewable by non-staff. Cleaning services or technicians that access your building should not be able to view patient files in plain sight.

- Keep all paperwork and reports face down and secure from unauthorized access.

- Do not post the practitioner or the therapist schedule in public areas which are accessible to non-staff.

- Ensure signed authorization is required for therapy notes except to the therapist providing the treatment.

- Ensure signed authorization is required for any disclosure to employers, schools, or other institutions for any patient participation.

- Ensure signed authorization is required for disclosure of any marketing, fundraising, or insurers for billing, etc.

- Utilize shredding devices for disposal of notes, papers, and memos.

- Do not leave documents on copiers and fax machines.

Information Technology IT Provider

In addition to building a culture of privacy and confidentiality, there are also specific steps to request from your information technology provider. Use this list below:

1. **Passwords:** Implement a complete password protection policy. Access to all equipment containing PHI should be carefully monitored and password protected. Check your Windows or MacBook for how to setup good complex passwords. It is common to invest in biometric devices like fingerprint readers and set up 2

factor authentication for access to software and applications that display PHI.

2. **Business Associates Agreement (BAA):** Require all your vendors that have access to your patients' PHI to sign and provide you with a full BAA agreement. Explain that under HIPAA and HITECH laws, they are covered entities and need to sign their acknowledgment and agreement of patient privacy rules. This is for all vendors that provide you software, legal advice, billing, scheduling, etc. If they are unwilling to sign, then find alternate vendors.

3. **Secure Your Email:** Switch your current email provider to an HIPAA and HITECH secure email provider. All your emails should be fully secured and encrypted. All data must be encrypted and protected.

4. **Encrypted Document**: Use file and document encryption software. Equipment like laptops, phones, and tablets with PHI Protected Health Information are more secure than paperwork and notebooks but they can also be misplaced and lost. A secure file and document encryption program will protect from unauthorized access. Even USB flash drives can and should be encrypted or require fingerprint scanners to access.

5. **Data Backup:** Require your managed services provider (MSP) to prove that data is being backed up and encrypted. There has to be full

contingency planning and all data recovery and restoration should be fully documented by your MSP or IT providers. Cloud is an option but restoration of data takes longer through many cloud providers.

6. **Privacy:** Respect patient privacy by having them provide specific signed forms that allow you to contact them at work. Use patient coded ID instead of full names and discuss communication protocols so that unnecessary information is not leaked.

7. **Wi-Fi:** Secure your wireless network and use a strong password. Wireless networks are easily hacked.

8. **Anti-Virus and Anti-Malware:** Request that your MSP keep your software patches up-to-date and install the latest anti-virus and anti-malware software to keep your computers from unauthorized hacking. Special wireless routers and firewalls equipment will be required to fully secure from unauthorized hacking.

9. **Log:** All vendors and others that receive patient PHI should be carefully logged. Document the date, time, who might have access and for what purpose.

10. **Document:** Create a document and keep it up-to-date with all your efforts in complying with HITECH and HIPAA. This include courses that you and your staff have attended.

Examples

Here are some real life examples of what can happen when a health care provider has gaps in their IT security.

A group of cardiologists used a publicly accessible Internet-based calendar to post patients' surgical and clinical appointments for many years. They did not even implement the most basic HIPAA requirements and they were required to pay $100,000 in fines.[37]

A Respiratory Therapist in Ohio accessed 596 records with confidential patient information over a 10-month period. Although she was allowed access to the patients she was treating, she abused her access because she also viewed the data of patients she was not treating. She is facing possible jail time. [38]

Sending a patient's overdue bill to a **collection agency** can also violate HIPAA requirements because of the bill contains confidential information.[39]

All the above suggestions are relatively inexpensive and allow your practice to be prepared. This preparation and implementation of security protocol is a powerful way to communicate to your patients and their families that your therapy

---

[37] https://www.aappublications.org/news/2016/10/13/HIT101316
[38] https://www.hipaajournal.com/respiratory-therapist-convicted-criminal-hipaa-violations-3486/
[39] https://healthitsecurity.com/news/nj-psychologist-to-fight-hipaa-violation-allegations

practice is progressive, up-to-date and most importantly, cyber safe for them.

About the Author

Amjad & Imtiaz Khanmohamed have experience with inventory, warehousing, and customers in multiple industries including: beauty supply, janitorial supply, industrial equipment, building materials, electrical equipment, medical equipment, packaging, lighting, and furniture.

They know the business processes and they have an eye for efficiency. They help CEOs and business owners gain a better view of their own operations – better visibility means better control, opening the doors for collaboration across departments, reducing operational costs, and increasing cash flow.

They can guarantee they will improve your bottom line. They will work with your team to identify processes that could be improved, with no contract and no strings - a free consultation. They're confident you'll see a 300% return on your investment in the first year, because they've done it for more organizations in more industries than they can count.

Schedule a call here:
https://www.aiminsight.com/schedule.html

How to Recover From a Cybersecurity Breach

By Robert Magio

The following is a true story from a recent client:

"I was driving to work this morning when I received a frantic call from my office manager. 'Tom, we've been hacked; they took all our computer files,' Janice said with panic in her voice. Within 5 minutes I arrived at the office. Everyone seemed to be in a state of confusion, huddled around a computer monitor.

I walked over and saw a red screen and a timer counting down. 'Your files have been encrypted,' it said in poorly written English and Russian. "Your data will be deleted unless the ransom of 10 BTC is paid within 36 hours."

We quickly discovered the thieves also had our financial information and data on all our clients. Calls started to come in slowly from our clients telling our staff that we've been sending them spam all morning."

As shocking as it may sound, this is just one of many common scenarios that I hear about all the time. For over 15 years, I have been helping the leaders of small and medium sized businesses leverage technology to improve profitability and reduce risk. I am the COO of CR Computer, one of New York's highest-rated technology management companies. I am also the founder of Never Breached, a leading provider of cybersecurity and compliance solutions for small and medium sized businesses.

Too many businesses fall victim to cybercrime, but there is hope. In this chapter, I will discuss two things: first, the seven critical actions our security experts recommend when a business is recovering from this type of attack and, second, five unexpected steps you can take right now to protect your business before a breach occurs.

How Does a Breach Occur?

A cybersecurity breach is the intrusion of a criminal element into a computer/network with the intention of destroying and/or stealing sensitive computer data. You might be surprised to discover how easy it is to become a victim of a cybersecurity breach. Here are some real-life examples:

- An office manager accidentally clicking a malicious website link in a spam email.

- A sales manager opening a fake quote approval email attachment that contains malware.

- An executive assistant visiting a phony website and unintentionally giving their passwords to Russian hackers.

- The head of human resources being fooled into sending corporate bank account details to a criminal posing as the CEO, who later empties the company's operating account.

You may have heard similar stories in the news, the question is: What do you do next?

Responding to a Breach: Different Scenarios Require Different Responses

Cybersecurity breaches can be immediate or lurk within your system for months. An attack can take nanoseconds to occur and then, in the case of a ransomware infection, it can launch a devastating attack immediately, and without warning. Or, a stealthier villain could inject malware that collects information and keystrokes while lurking undetected in your network for months. IBM estimates it takes companies an average of 206 days to realize there has even been a hack.[40] Imagine the amount of damage that can occur in that time!

Therefore, depending on what type of security incident has occurred, you will need to take different actions to deal with it. I have tried to take

---

[40] https://newsroom.ibm.com/2019-07-23-IBM-Study-Shows-Data-Breach-Costs-on-the-Rise-Financial-Impact-Felt-for-Years

this variety into account with the following list of responses:

1. ISOLATE: If you have been hit with malware, a virus, or a ransomware attack, disconnect the affected computer(s) from the internet and/or network. Malware and viruses like to spread, so try to isolate them as much as possible.

2. PRESERVE: Do NOT scan the computer for viruses. If this is a serious breach, a scan could destroy important forensics data or the loss of ransomware keys that could impact the ability to recover from the event.

3. WAIT: If this is a ransomware attack wherein thieves hold computers or data hostage in exchange for money, do not pay the ransom right away, as there is no guarantee the criminals will return the data once you pay them. Contact a cybersecurity professional to assist and advise.

4. CHANGE YOUR PASSWORDS: Always change your passwords. Even if the breach was simply malware-related, every password should be changed. This includes passwords for: computers, emails, any routers or other "smart" devices on the network, even online banking and shopping. Any vulnerable devices should be removed. You may want to hire a cybersecurity firm to do an overall assessment of your system and recommend additional layers of protection.

5. NOTIFY: If the incident included a breach of customer information, you may require cyber forensic analysis. Each state has different laws regarding the procedure for alerting an organization's affected customers. After talking with your cybersecurity expert, you may want to talk to a lawyer, as notification may need to occur within 72 hours of discovery.

6. TRAIN: Alert your employees to the breach and implement safeguards/protocols to prevent it from happening again. This should include mandatory training for the entire company (including C-level staff) and regular cybersecurity testing.

7. BACKUP: You need to have a comprehensive backup strategy in place that is tested on a regular basis. You should also consider the creation of a business continuity and\or disaster recovery (BC/DR) plan. However, planning is not enough, you also need to test and drill your plan periodically.

The Costs of Recovering from a Cybersecurity Breach

Consider these costs for an affected company:

- The average cost of a data breach is $3.92 million dollars.[41]

- The average ransomware attack costs $133,000.[42]

---

[41] https://newsroom.ibm.com/2019-07-23-IBM-Study-Shows-Data-Breach-Costs-on-the-Rise-Financial-Impact-Felt-for-Years
[42] https://www.varonis.com/blog/cybersecurity-statistics

- 43% of cyberattacks target small businesses.[43]

- A jaw-dropping 60% of small companies breached go bankrupt within six months.[44]

If you have a systems backup, you may be able to restore operations with minimal downtime. If you handle it carefully and professionally, your company's reputation will be able to recover from the damage. If you have cyber insurance (which is a very good idea), you may be able to receive monetary compensation for the losses, as long as you can prove you were diligent in protecting your company and clients from a cybersecurity breach.

It's All About Prevention

As you can see, a cybersecurity breach can be devastating to a company's bottom line, let alone a company's very existence. Yet, many companies are shockingly still unprepared. A recent survey of 4,100 businesses conducted by a Chicago insurance company found that seven out of 10 had no plans in place at all.[45]

Are you prepared? Here are a few things I suggest implementing immediately to reduce your exposure:

---

[43] https://enterprise.verizon.com/resources/executivebriefs/2019-dbir-executive-brief-emea.pdf

[44] https://www.sec.gov/news/statement/cybersecurity-challenges-for-small-midsize-businesses.html

[45] https://www.inc.com/adam-levin/more-than-70-percent-of-businesses-admit-theyre-unprepared-for-a-cyberattack.html

1. PASSWORDS: Use strong passwords and two-factor authentication, the latter of which requires users to receive a one-time code on a separate device to gain access. This is a strongly recommended second layer of protection. As malware on mobile continues to rise, restrict smartphone access as much as possible or consider issuing your own company phones if the level of security is warranted for your industry.

2. EMAIL SECURITY: Protect/enhance your email. According to Verizon, the most common method hackers use to gain access is sending phony emails (phishing), which accounts for 94% of malware attacks.[46] The fact is, 95% of breaches are due to human error; you can see how the inbox is a company's weakest link.[47] Therefore, it is strongly recommended that you have a robust email security program that can potentially flag and/or isolate suspicious emails before someone clicks on them. Today's email security solutions use cloud servers and AI to outsmart spammers, while reducing false positives.

3. TRAIN AND TEST: Create strong in-house policies that include incident reporting, along with disaster drills and even covert testing. If a cybersecurity breach occurs, does everyone know what to do or to whom they should report the issue? After mandatory employee training/testing,

---

[46] https://enterprise.verizon.com/resources/executivebriefs/2019-dbir-executive-brief-emea.pdf

[47] https://www.securitymagazine.com/articles/85601-of-successful-security-attacks-are-the-result-of-human-error

you should regularly run real-world simulations to see how quickly everyone can respond. (After all, a cyber breach can be just as devastating as a fire or earthquake.) Finally, you may want to utilize a phishing simulator—a program designed to send phony emails to employees. If someone clicks on a link, instead of triggering a virus, the admin is alerted. This can give you an overall assessment of your company's preparedness.

4. BACKUP: Have a reliable, secure backup for your data. In earlier years, tape backups and removable hard drives were quite common; today, however, smart companies opt for hybrid backup systems that house servers both in the office and synchronize to the cloud. These backups are faster and more robust. Some prefer a cloud-only method; whichever method you prefer, a backup can exponentially reduce downtime and damages.

5. WORK WITH PROFESSIONALS: Hire a professional computer security firm. In many cases contracting with a 3rd party is now the law. A good cyber policy has many moving parts and the best option is to choose a firm that can oversee the entire program. You'll worry less and be able to focus on your business.

A cybersecurity breach is one of the worst things that can happen, and many companies are just one click away from disaster. Don't wait until it's too late—when hackers have already broken in and stole your data. We recommend you find a competent cybersecurity management company and begin protecting your future as soon as possible.

If you'd like to learn more go to www.Never Breached.com/25things and download our 25-Point Cybersecurity Checklist. Our list is specifically designed to help business owners make better decisions on the safety of their network and data.

About the Author

Robert Magio is a technology expert who empowers business leaders to leverage technology so they can accelerate their growth and reduce their corporate risk.

Often referred to as a tech genius, Robert began his technical career at 16 years old, working at Citibank with their computer support team. Growing up in the technology industry, Robert has worked directly with the executives of major brands such as AOL, Time Warner, *Health Magazine* and many more, assisting them in optimizing and securing their computer technology.

Today, Robert works directly with the executives of small and medium sized businesses in New York, helping them use technology to grow and secure their businesses.

If you are interested in working with Robert and his team of experts at CR Computer, you can reach them at crcomputer.com.

CPSIA information can be obtained
at www.ICGtesting.com
Printed in the USA
LVHW031611050420
652287LV00008B/560